Breathing
NEW LIFE
into
LENT

Library of Congress Cataloging-in-Publication Data
Breathing new life into Lent : a collection of creative worship
    resources / Robert E. Stowe ... [et al.].
        p.   cm.
    ISBN 0-8170-1319-9 (paperback
    1. Lent – Prayer-books and devotions – English. 2. Lenten sermons.
3. Easter service. 4. Easter – Sermons. 5. Sermons, American.
6. Liturgies.   I. Stowe, Robert E.
BV85.B665   1999
264 – dc21
                                                        98-43639

Printed in the U.S.A.
06   05   04   03   02   01   00   99
  6   5   4   3   2   1

Contents

About the Authors vii

Revised Common Lectionary Readings, Year A viii

Preface ix

Section One: **WORSHIP SERVICES** 1

Introduction 3

Ash Wednesday 4

First Sunday in Lent 7

Second Sunday in Lent 10

Third Sunday in Lent 13

Fourth Sunday in Lent 16

Fifth Sunday in Lent 19

Palm Sunday 22

Maundy Thursday 25

Easter Sunday 30

Section Two: **PRAYER DIALOGUES AND ANTIPHONAL HYMNS** . . . 33

Introduction 35

Ash Wednesday 36

First Sunday in Lent 38

Second Sunday in Lent 40

Third Sunday in Lent 42

Fourth Sunday in Lent 44

Fifth Sunday in Lent 46

Palm Sunday / Passion Sunday 48

Maundy Thursday 50

Easter Sunday 52

Section Three: LENTEN REFLECTIONS 55

 Introduction   57

 General Lenten Reflections   58

 Ash Wednesday   60

 First Sunday in Lent   61

 Second Sunday in Lent   62

 Third Sunday in Lent   63

 Fourth Sunday in Lent   64

 Fifth Sunday in Lent   66

 Palm Sunday / Passion Sunday   67

 Maundy Thursday   69

 Easter Sunday   70

Section Four: NEW SONGS FOR LENT 71

 Introduction   73

 Born Anew   74

 Healing Seasons   76

 Roll the Stone Away   78

 Stone and Bread   80

 Will You Wash My Feet?   82

 Your People   83

About the Authors

ROBERT E. STOWE is pastor of the First Congregational Church in Ashfield, Massachusetts. He is author of *The Love Feast*, a two-day retreat plan focusing on meals and the Bible.

DONNA E. SCHAPER is Associate Conference Minister for the United Church of Christ. She has written several books, including *Calmly Plotting the Resurrection* (United Church Press).

ANNE McKINSTRY is a hymn writer and poet who resides in Lee, Massachusetts.

JANET E. POWERS is a United Church of Christ minister and lifelong musician.

Revised Common Lectionary
Readings, Year A

Readings for the Season of Lent through Easter Sunday

Ash Wednesday

Joel 2:1–2, 12–17 or Isaiah 58:1–12
Psalm 51:1–17
2 Corinthians 5:20b–6:10
Matthew 6:1–6, 16–21

First Sunday in Lent

Genesis 2:15–17, 3:1–7
Psalm 32
Romans 5:12–19
Matthew 4:1–11

Second Sunday in Lent

Genesis 12:1–4a
Psalm 121
Romans 4:1–5, 13–17
John 3:1–17 or Matthew 17:1–9

Third Sunday in Lent

Exodus 17:1–7
Psalm 95
Romans 5:1–11
John 4:5–42

Fourth Sunday in Lent

1 Samuel 16:1–13
Psalm 23
Ephesians 5:8–14
John 9:1–41

Fifth Sunday in Lent

Ezekiel 37:1–14
Psalm 130
Romans 8:6–11
John 11:1–45

Palm/Passion Sunday

Matthew 21:1–11
Psalm 118:1–2, 19–29

Maundy Thursday

Exodus 12:1–4 (5–10), 11–14
Psalm 116:1–2, 12–19
1 Corinthians 11:23–26
John 13:1–17, 31b–35

Easter Sunday

Acts 10:34–43 or Jeremiah 31:1–6
Psalm 118:1–2, 14–24
Colossians 3:1–4 or Acts 10:34–43
John 20:1–18 or Matthew 28:1–10

Preface

Breathing New Life into Lent: A Collection of Creative Worship Resources contains a rich selection of innovative ideas for worship during the Lenten season. However, the book's four contributors — Rev. Robert E. Stowe, Ms. Anne McKinstry, Rev. Donna E. Schaper, and Rev. Janet E. Powers — have only one goal: to serve churches in their efforts to make worship during Lent as fulfilling and enriching as possible.

In addition to offering ideas for the standard liturgical elements of nine worship services, from Ash Wednesday through Easter Sunday, this resource includes Lenten reflections, original Lenten songs, and a lyrical new genre for worship: the prayer dialogue, based on antiphonal scripture readings (Section Two).

Breathing New Life into Lent is appropriate for all churches, but those who follow the Revised Common Lectionary will find it particularly useful as the resources are based on the readings from Lectionary Year A (see p. viii). Pastors and worship leaders are invited to read through this resource and to use as much or as little as they deem appropriate for their local worship setting. Some congregations might choose to ground an entire Lenten program in these resources, while other churches will merely select an occasional song, prayer, story, or sermon idea from the collection.

Again, the goal of this book is to serve, not to limit. In that regard, the authors and the staff at Judson Press hope that this resource will serve as a springboard for greater creativity in worship and that the ideas contained herein will truly breathe new life into your Lenten season.

Breathing New Life into Lent honors the traditional tone of Lent while exploring the season's vitality in new ways. Lent is not just about confronting and confessing our capacity for evil and repenting of our sin. Lent is also concerned with recognizing God's goodness and the Spirit's activity in amending our lives. Yes, we must allow Lent to plumb our depths, to convict our hearts. However, we must hear as well the redemptive word from God, proclaiming renewed life for humanity and all of creation.

The authors have adopted a word to express how God seeks to transform our living. We call it *reframing*. The primary goal of Lent is to reframe us. By *reframe*, we mean Lent offers us a different picture of life, of who we are and who God is. As an example of how Lent reframes our lives, Robert Stowe recounts this story:

> Walking across the church lawn to Easter Sunday worship over twenty years ago, Harland Lewis taught me how to understand Easter. Harland G. Lewis was the senior pastor of the First Congregational Church in Farmington, Connecticut; I was his young associate. I was lamenting the many people who would fill the sanctuary that morning and then disappear until next Christmas — or perhaps not until next year's Easter service. Harland advised me, "Bob, what I have learned over the years is it is not we who defend Easter, but Easter which defends us."

His insight reframed Easter for me. Since then, I have come to understand that Christianity is not about pastors or dedicated laypeople bringing the gospel message to the world; Lent is not about cleaning our spiritual houses; Easter is not to be staked out as the pivotal holy day of the year, its profound truth captured, and its treasure guarded. Christianity and the holy days of Lent and Easter are not about protecting God. They are about how God protects and renews us at our cores.

Lent is God's time to initiate change in us. Its beauty and mystery set the stage for Easter's triumph. Lent, therefore, is not about human activity; it is about God preparing us for resurrection. Lent is a time to create for ourselves a holy openness to profound transformation.

Lent refashions how we look at ourselves and how we look at God. From beginning to end, Lent is a season of God's activity. Nothing more clearly signals that than the Gospel reading on the first Sunday in Lent.

Jesus is in the wilderness. The devil tempts him. Jesus rejects Evil's temptation. There is no human activity here. God in Jesus actively refutes and refuses the devil's sophisticated ploys. We make a grave spiritual mistake if we pretend that we can mimic Jesus, mouth his words, and expect evil to evaporate. Resist evil; fight it tooth and nail, but never pretend we can so easily banish it as Jesus does.

Lent's other Gospel readings teem with claims God makes for us and upon our lives. However, in each case, God's actions set up the possibility for human participation. These lessons picture an active God teasing, cajoling, and demanding movement in our lives. At times that movement is towards change and healing, but that change and healing are created by God for us and not something we coax into existence.

Therefore, from Ash Wednesday to the foundation-shaking event of Easter, God works to bring us a wholeness of which we are bereft. This is salvation. Our contribution is creating holy holes in our lives to accommodate God's wholeness. We create those holes in private spiritual disciplines and devotions and in vibrant corporate worship services. Yet, it is God who delightfully fills those holes, pouncing on us with the tear-stopping cataclysm of Easter. Welcome to our journey toward that joyous calamity. May *Breathing New Life into Lent* become a treasured assistant blowing new vitality into your worship services.

Section One

WORSHIP SERVICES

For Rev. Charles P. Luckey Jr.
whose sense of play infuses me;

For Rev. Harland G. Lewis
whose dignity inspires me;

&

For Dr. Benjamin F. Kimpel
whose soaring intelligence informs my own;

Precious and beloved — always treasured.

— R.E.S.

Introduction

In this section, Rev. Robert E. Stowe provides the essential elements of nine worship services, beginning with Ash Wednesday and concluding with Easter Sunday. Each service includes a call to worship; corporate prayers of praise and confession; offertory prayer; and prayer of thanksgiving, intercession, and petition; as well as suggestions for a sermon theme. Most services also include a children's sermon. These elements may be used in whole or in part, according to your worship needs and style.

Note that the calls to worship are responsive readings where the leader's voice is in a regular typeface and the people's response is in **boldface** type. Where the leader and people are to respond in unison, the reading is prefaced with "ALL" and appears in ***bold and italic typeface.***

Ash Wednesday

Gospel Reading: Matthew 6:1–6, 16–21

CALL TO WORSHIP
[based on Psalm 51]

Have mercy on us, O God, according to your steadfast love; according to your abundant mercy blot out our transgressions.

You can and do erase our moral and spiritual debts. You cancel any thoughts you have of judging us harshly.

Wash us thoroughly from our iniquities and cleanse us from our sin.

On our own, we can not clean our consciences. We are unable to scrub away our own mistakes and live guilt free.

ALL: *Therefore, we turn to you, our only Source, for freedom from past faults. We appeal to you for renewal and new life. We begin by praising you.*

PRAYER OF PRAISE [unison]

God, whom we call Father/Mother, we adore you. You ease our way back into your arms. You give us prayer, fasting, weeping, and torn hearts as means by which we may return to you. You call our brokenness, wholeness. In your slow anger and hurried love, you forge a way to happiness. Glory to you who raises us to blessing and bounty. You are holy and wonderful. Amen.

PRAYER OF CONFESSION [unison]

We tremble at your approach. We cower before your purity. We collapse before the onslaught of your holiness. For we, dear God, have stood tall in arrogance. We have raised ourselves high in lust for human approval. We have feigned a stature built on false premises and tarnished living. Forgive us. Ground us in your greater realities and higher demands. Humble us through spiritual disciplines. Bring us low so that you may raise us to heights we cannot ascend by effort or merit.

CHILDREN'S SERMON: Explaining the Ritual of Ashes

[Bring ashes to put on the children's foreheads. You may have saved the ashes burnt from the previous year's palms, or burn some newspapers or leaves at home and bring in those ashes.]

Ask the children: Where have you seen ashes before? Where do ashes come from? How do we make ashes?

[Fire. The children may have seen cigarette ashes or campfire ashes; some may know that cremation reduces people's bodies to ashes.]

In our religion, ashes have a long important history. For example, in the Hebrew Scriptures, people rubbed ashes on themselves when they realized they had disobeyed God. They believed that if they were deeply sorry for what they had done, God would give them new lives. Putting ashes on themselves was a way to show they were sorry.

Look at the ashes I brought with me tonight. Tonight we place ashes on our foreheads in the sign of the cross. By doing this we remember that out of the ashes of Jesus' death, God brought new life. We remind ourselves that one very important way to reconnect with God is to admit how we have tried to live apart from God. By reminding ourselves that we fail God, we let God return to our lives and start our lives all over again. [Place the ashes on any foreheads of the children willing to do the ritual; give them a choice and don't pressure any who are unwilling.]

SERMON NOTES

Main Point: Exhort your congregation to pious disciplines this Ash Wednesday. Address the need for and efficacy of private devotional practices; propose specific examples of how people can energize their faith by practicing one or more of the disciplines during Lent.

Charity, prayer, and fasting are private occupations, not public spectacles. The way in which we embrace them is as important as doing them at all. Matthew makes this clear in today's scripture passage. He took great exception to the public piety flaunted openly in his time.

Our generation is not one of public, let alone much private piety. How do we connect with Matthew's message? Is it best to bypass the issue as inappropriate to our situation? I would argue that, in an age of decreasing personal Christian religious expression and increasing interest in other spiritual experiences, Ash Wednesday and Lent are shortchanged if issues of personal spiritual growth are not addressed. But how?

In mainstream Christianity, we tend to discuss things to death. In contrast, in this text, God talks about action, about penitence put into motion. Perhaps, the discussion groups your church forms during Lent might adopt one or more of these disciplines to flesh out your conversations. You might use this sermon to summon your people to the disciplines of charity, prayer, and fasting we have ignored. Exhort your congregation as a group and as individuals to undertake these disciplines during Lent — and practice them yourself.

For example, look at charity. Suggest that people might benefit from a new approach to charity. Jesus tells us to do it secretly, without expecting recognition or reward. Encourage willing individuals to grow through the discipline of charity during Lent. Have them plan what time, treasure, or talent they will give, and whether they will do so on a daily or weekly basis. Encourage them to act out this discipline *quietly*.

Forget the tax implications and record keeping for a change. They might make an anonymous cash donation, or they could put in an evening's work at a soup kitchen in a neighboring town where no one knows them.

Feel free to make suggestions, but let the people decide how to conduct their own experiments in charity, prayer, and fasting. Provide resources such as selected Bible readings and an annotated bibliography that might help them engage practically and spiritually in these actions. Urge them to keep journals to record their own reflections and impressions of the experience; when the Lenten season draws to a close, encourage them to read through their thoughts and prayers and observe how God has changed them. By giving more of themselves away and by doing it in secret, what do they sense returning to them? Perhaps more important than anything else, make sure you adopt one of the disciplines for yourself — in secret. Resist the temptation to share your own results later with the congregation in a sermon.

OFFERTORY PRAYER

Here we are, Lord. Send us — first, to our knees, admitting how we have left you out of our lives — and then to our rooms to secretly pray not only for ourselves but also for your wide, wooly world, which so wholly ignores you. Finally, send us into that world to tell it about the slowness of your anger and quickness of your love. Amen.

PRAYER OF THANKSGIVING, INTERCESSION, & PETITION

We thank you for mistakes: both the small ones we ignore and the big, juicy ones that splatter our lives with guilt and shame. We thank you for how our mistakes prompt us to repair broken relationships. We thank you for how our mistakes invite us to renew our relationship with you. Above all, we thank you for returning us to strength through weakness.

We pray for a flawed and faltering world. We ask that your presence invade people who ignore or deny you. We pray for people who live along the thin line of "me first and me only," for people whose spirituality boils down to a tax write-off or prayer seized only on occasions of panic, and for people whose ideas of self-importance are built upon fame, honor, or public recognition. For these people we pray for new life. We ask that they may hear and heed your call to renewal. Let them discover the treasures of compassion, humility, and personal devotion to you, the Source of our lives.

We pray these things for others because we know how much we need them, too. We pray for the blessing of ashes: a simple sign of an interior orientation to tender truth-telling about ourselves and of a parched longing for your rivers of renewal. Fill our journeys in Lent with quiet acts and private resuscitations. Throughout this season, remind us of our unbearable frailty and the unrelenting offer of strength you extend to us.

First Sunday in Lent

Gospel Reading: Matthew 4:1–11

CALL TO WORSHIP
[based on Psalm 32, Jerusalem Bible]

Happy are they whose fault is forgiven, whose sin is blotted out.

God says, "Before I poured life into you, I created a stunning being full of promise and good. Before you took babysteps, I forgave your first errors and all since."

Happy are those whom Yahweh accuses of no guilt, whose spirits are incapable of deceit.

So, we, walkers on God's way, come here. We come to worship, to empty ourselves of worry and guilt, asking the Lord to return us to the goodness with which God made us. May our spirits pool together in this prayer.

PRAYER OF PRAISE [unison]

Holy God, you create many worlds. Among them are ecosystems and star systems, microbiology and macroeconomics. Then, you inseparably tie human life to them. Their life nurtures ours. We protect and nourish them. Finally, you set before us life and death: trust versus guile; faithful work versus convenience. We praise you who favors life. We bless you who confronts and contains evil. Amen.

PRAYER OF CONFESSION [unison]

As with good clothes that we toss away, so we shed our trust in you. We abandon innocence. Our striving is vain ambition. We count on knowledge to save us, cleverness to protect us, and our own authority to banish evil from among us. Forgive us. Turn us to the life abundant that you lay at our feet. May an incomparable sense of your presence flow through us.

CHILDREN'S SERMON: Jesus Gets into an Argument

What is an argument? Have you ever been in an argument? How did you feel about it? [Give the children a chance to respond.]

In today's Gospel reading, Jesus gets into an argument. It is a very serious argument. He argues with the devil. The Evil One is trying to get Jesus to do things Jesus knows are wrong.

Sometimes, when I get into an argument, I find it hard to figure out who is wrong and who is right. How can you tell if the person with whom you are arguing is wrong? [Let the children try to answer.] What are some of the things you think the devil tries to get people to do that are wrong?

In this time we call Lent, we focus on looking at evil and how it appears in our lives. We think and pray about the things we are doing that aren't right. We ask God to teach us how to spot evil when it gets close to us, and we ask the Lord to help us fight it. We learn from Jesus, who said "no" when the Evil One tried to get him to do things he knew were wrong. Like Jesus, we hope to defeat evil.

Our Bibles can help us in this problem with evil. Sometimes, Scripture provides us with clues to what is right and good when we are confused. If those of us who have Bibles will read them and remember the stories like the one we heard today, and if we ask God to help us understand what those stories mean for our lives, then hopefully, when the devil tempts us, we will be able to say "no" the way Jesus did.

SERMON NOTES

Main Point: Reconsider how we look at evil and how it operates. Evil's real power is not in getting us to do something we know is wrong. Its chief ploy is to get us to do something that could very easily seem right, but isn't.

Evil is not stupid. It cleverly masks itself in wars between ideas. For us, that warfare is often waged internally within our minds. In today's lesson, we can see an example of that warfare out in the open. In Jesus' exchange with the devil, evil powerfully imbeds itself in intellectual discourse. The skirmish with Jesus occurs in the greatest intellectual forum of the day — that is, in the interpretation of biblical passages. The Evil One uses Scripture to try to convince Jesus to do something. Then, Jesus counters with another biblical passage to resist. You might make detailed comments about each of the three temptations and how Jesus reframes the devil's carefully masked distortions of truth.

On the other hand, you could deal with the very real problem of how we sift through apparently equal, but conflicting claims. For example, in social issues, we have debates over the death penalty, just war, and trickle-down versus bottom-up economics. In religion, we clash over issues of biblical interpretation — about male-female gender roles, homosexuality, and literal versus contextual interpretation of Scripture. Think and pray about how we can use the Bible humbly. How can we hold to our beliefs without arrogance or condescension? How can we carry God's truth and remain humble enough to realize that far more important than how we interpret Scripture is how Scripture interprets us?

We also face the dilemma of how to respond to those with whom we contend. Jesus vanquishes the devil and moves on, but if we are to love our enemies as Christ urges us, how do we love people whose social, political, or religious views conflict with our own?

OFFERTORY PRAYER [unison]

Here we are. Send us — into the deserts of ours and others' lives, supported by your truth, held upright and not uptight by your Spirit. Take us and use us as you would. May our lives bear your simple truths to others, yet may we never be unbearable to those to whom you send us. Amen.

PRAYER OF THANKSGIVING, INTERCESSION, & PETITION

We thank you, God, for our journeys on the paths of wisdom and wit. By your wisdom, we are able to discern evil's silky seductions. By our wits, we know these seductions are too strong for us to manage alone. Thank you for being present with us through your wisdom and in our wits.

We pray for places where evil has broken into human living. We pray for struggles on biological levels where evil enslaves people chemically. We pray for struggles on economic levels where greed imprisons both rich and poor. We pray for the struggles on personal levels, where evil heaps people with problems until life becomes an aching burden.

Finally, we pray for ourselves. Place us on the high, holy highway of Lent, which runs straight through the wilderness of our lives. Where we have basic unmet needs, supply us first with your truth about us and our needs. Then, meet those needs but only to the point that abundance does not overwhelm us. May we grow through our hungers, learn from our temptations to independence and power, and rebuke all worship of any thing or power less than you. Amen.

LENTEN DOXOLOGY

MAY BE SUNG TO THE TUNE OF "OLD HUNDREDTH" OR TO VARIOUS ALTERED RHYTHMS, SUCH AS "MORNING HYMN."

> Bless God for whom we're meant to be
> Released, cut loose, from all sin free.
> Water that lives, food brought to earth,
> You bring life through your Spirit's birth.
> Amen.

Second Sunday in Lent

Gospel Reading: John 3:1–17

CALL TO WORSHIP

[based on Psalm 121]

We lift our eyes to the hills. Yet, our help comes from the Lord who keeps our lives.

God keeps our going out and our coming in. God births, blesses, and rebirths us.

ALL: *God, like a woman in labor, sweats over our spiritual births. The Spirit pushes hard against our resistance. Then, divine delight soars at our newly birthed life.*

PRAYER OF PRAISE [unison]

We praise you who never grows old but who is always new and fresh in our lives. With spittle, dust, and the breath of your Spirit, you give us life. Then, you call us to abandon dead ends and shuck stale living, and you promise us life born anew. Finally, when our earth's journeys end, you draw us out from death into life and light again. Bless you, constant Creator. Bless you, joyful Jesus. Bless you, sacred and surprising Spirit. Amen.

PRAYER OF CONFESSION [unison]

Forgive us, wind-ripping Spirit. We refuse transformation. We sink back while you call us out. We name what is habit right. We muster false hope that all will be well. Yet, all is well only when our life proceeds from you. Forgive and change us. Blow away the cobwebs of our conventions. Join us to the new life breathed into the world through Jesus our Christ. Within our hearts, blossom the flowers of your Realm.

CHILDREN'S SERMON: Giving Birth

[Have pictures on hand of babies — human infants of different races and animal babies as well.]

Ask: Do any of you have a new baby in your family? [Get input from those children who have. You might ask for the newborns' names or how these children feel about the new baby.]

In today's Bible story, Jesus tells an old man, Nicodemus, that after we are born by our mother, all of us need to be born a second time. Nicodemus listens politely, but he doesn't understand what Jesus is saying. He thinks Jesus is saying he has to become a little baby again, and that sounds crazy! Nicodemus doesn't realize that Jesus is talking in word pictures, to help us understand something about God. Jesus was trying to explain that when we decide to follow him, we have to become a new person — like a new baby who has to learn everything from the beginning. Only when we become like new babies in Jesus, God is our parent, and our new life comes from the Spirit, who teaches us how to laugh and love and trust God.

SERMON NOTES

Main Point: Rather than identifying with Nicodemus, emphasize Jesus' call for us to be born anew, and explore what that means to us.

This approach skips lightly past Nicodemus. Instead, focus on the idea of being born from God's presence, which has drawn near in the person of Jesus. In taking this approach, avoid the heavy, finger-pointing hand that pretends to know precisely what Jesus meant by saying we must be "born again" of the Spirit. To presume to know exactly what God meant seems arrogant to me. Yes, Jesus' insistence on Spirit-birth is fundamental to our faith. However, the tone with which we proclaim that belief is everything. If we claim to know the ways and means of the blowing, shuddering Spirit of God, then we begin to trample mystery into the margins of our religious life. On the other hand, if we can personally feel Jesus' insistence on this birth and communicate it with honesty as well as with trepidation, then we better approach the Lenten spirit.

Among the timeless treasures in this passage is Christ's assurance that it is never too late for anyone — person, church, or nation — to be reborn in his Spirit. For those whose personal devotional practices are waning, for the many clergy and lay folk struggling with the future of our mainline churches, for the woman just tagged with a speeding ticket that means the loss of her license, for the man who hopes the doctor's new pill will tame the tension wracking his body — this assurance is not merely good news; it is *great* news. Preach this treasure — that it is never too late to be born again into the Spirit. Preach it because we badly need to hear it, but preach it in ways that will lead us to crumble into the welcoming arms of a nurturing God. Lent is not about armoring ourselves with the right faith. Lent is about dissolving before the faithful One who births us anew.

OFFERTORY PRAYER

Here we are. Send us into your cluttered, clanging, confused world. Take and use us as you would. May your liquid, birth-bringing, exuberant Spirit burst open our lives. And may our lives bring that same Spirit to others.

PRAYER OF THANKSGIVING, INTERCESSION, & PETITION

We thank you, Spirit who crashes new life and wholeness where you will. We thank you for the surprising, unpredictable, untamable new life you spring upon us. We thank you for invading our muddle with new chances for life, day after day after day.

We pray for people whose lives slurry along. We pray for people who have given up on you, on themselves, on everything. We hold up to you folks who try to moderate your demands for renewal with compromise, delay, and rationalization. We pray for people enslaved by politeness, predictability, and planned living. Come to these people and pounce on their narrow expectations, forgotten dreams, and muted efforts to embrace you. Surprise them with the Spirit who sweeps new life into deadened places.

We pray for these people because when we pray for them, we pray for ourselves — because we know the same smallness of spirit. Confound us and confuse us until you crack us wide open to your new life. Where we are tummy tucked into security, rip us open. Then, flood our stapled lives with your life-renewing Spirit. Amen.

Third Sunday in Lent

Gospel Reading: John 4:5–42

CALL TO WORSHIP
[based on Psalm 95 and Exodus 17]

Today, may we listen for God's voice and not harden our hearts as Israel did at Meribah/Massah in the wilderness.

Meribah/Massah was yet another place where our ancestors tested God and quarreled. There, we treated God's presence as a means to our ends and not as an end in itself.

O come, let us sing to the Lord. Let us make a joyful noise to the rock of our salvation.

Instead of rebelling, let us worship and bow down before our Maker. We come into God's presence making joyful noise and giving God our praise.

PRAYER OF PRAISE [unison]

Holy Liquid Life, you are our wellspring, from whom joy, laughter, and purpose gush into our lives. You free us from dry places where life withers. You gently expand our narrow thinking. Then you guide the waters of your Spirit down the rocky river beds of our faith. Well of Life, we praise you! We adore you who quenches our cravings with the waters which banish thirst. Amen.

PRAYER OF CONFESSION [unison]

Our thinking, believing, and acting are dry wells. We panic when life becomes parched. We pant for convenience while we abandon the blessings of inconvenience. We search for life in ways it cannot be found. Forgive us, Holy God. Bring our minds and hearts back to your well and the fresh waters of your Spirit. Then, flood our lives with your Spirit and truth.

CHILDREN'S SERMON: Water & Food

[Bring crackers for the children.]

Ask: How do you know when you're hungry? When you get hungry, what do you want to eat? What are some of your favorite foods? [Remember some of them.] How many of you are hungry now? [Pass out one cracker to each child.]

In today's Bible reading, Jesus talks about both water and food. When he talks about food, however, he does not mean things such as [name some of their favorite foods]. He's talking in word pictures again. He says that the water God gives us is so good that the person who tastes it will never be thirsty again, and our favorite food should be doing what God wants us to do. That sounds pretty strange to us, but Jesus wasn't talking about the hunger that makes our stomachs growl. We are hungry and thirsty in our spirits, Jesus says, and the only way to satisfy that hunger is through an open relationship with God. For Jesus, God's food and water are very satisfying; they keep him strong and healthy in his spirit the same way our favorite foods keep our bodies strong and satisfied. Jesus gets this spiritual food from God and says that we can get it from him.

SERMON NOTES

Main Point: Focus on how neither rebellion in Exodus nor questioning in John prevents God from breaking into human lives to nourish us. Both scripture texts recognize the barrier-breaking prerogative of the Holy One. God's nature is to burst through all human barriers — rebellion, questioning, social strictures, et cetera.

There are luscious springs running through both Exodus and John's Gospel. Those springs flow from time-honored rocks. In Exodus, the rock is the one Moses struck at Horeb. In John, the rock is Jesus, out of whom water pours forth to slake our worst thirsts.

First, look at the rock in Exodus. Israel failed to trust God. Moses carefully underscores that this incident is not a religious triumph, but a failure. In spite of Israel's demands for water through testing and quarreling (the underlying import of the physical names Massah and Meribah), God breaks through the people's rebellion to supply the life-giving water anyway. It was a barrier-crashing divine prerogative.

Set against this text is John's rock in the person of Jesus. As he did with the woman who came to the well, Jesus may ask you to share your water with him. He wants to offer you his as well, but instead of accepting the gift, we quibble with Jesus, just as Israel did with Moses. We want Jesus, our Rock, pounded down into little, more manageable pieces. Like the woman, we "quarry" him, hoping he will answer us. From his answers, we hope to be able to build something that makes sense of our lives. For the woman from Sychar, this works. She gets answers that initiate a belief in Jesus.

More importantly, perhaps, in accepting the water Jesus offers, the woman puts down her jar, and the current of the strange, new, exciting water carries her onto a whole new path. The river of life flows from Jesus to the woman and on into her city.

You see, rocks can do anything. They can even gush with water for rebellious or uncomprehending people.

OFFERTORY PRAYER

Here we are, Lord. Send us into the wilderness where rocks promise water and water promises life. Take and use us as pitchers and pails, jugs and jars, buckets and barrels to carry your water into the world. Use us in quenching thirsts only you can satisfy. Amen.

PRAYER OF THANKSGIVING, INTERCESSION, & PETITION

We thank you, God who is river, rain, and ocean to us. For the many ways you quench our deepest thirsts, thank you. For people who love us and for meeting our basic needs, we thank you. Thank you for liquid insight and laughing faith. Above all, thank you for replenishing the dry places in our lives by the living water that you are.

We pray for people who are thirsty and who crave water. We pray especially for people facing drought, for people standing on life's shore feeling the tide has gone out, and for people who choose less than abundant life. For these and for others, we pray that you be their answers and refreshment.

Be the Life-Spring welling up in our lives, too. Wherever life leaves us chapped and chaffed, be our balm. Wherever our pails are empty, fill them. Pour into us a joy that spills out loose and free. Slosh us with a happiness we cannot gain or earn. Then, drown us in the life flooded with your Spirit, truth, and eternity. Amen.

Fourth Sunday in Lent

Gospel Reading: John 9:1–41

CALL TO WORSHIP

Our lives touch and are touched when we worship together.

We touch the persistent truths about ourselves — the truths about who we are and who we are not. Yet, we also touch the truth of who God means us to be and how God is even now at work in our lives.

Come, join me. Let our lives be changed. May we acknowledge all that blinds us and ask God for sight.

The things that blind us are many. Blaming others and ourselves cripples us. Our fears of success and failure close our eyes to the possibilities God wants to inject into our lives.

ALL: *Touching the truth about ourselves is not easy, but we come here to attempt exactly that. Being touched by you, Holy One, brings the life we need.*

PRAYER OF PRAISE [unison]

You are the Spirit who gives us sight into ourselves. God for whom blame is an obstacle to be crushed, you are endless optimism. You search among us not for hardened beliefs but for openings. You carve chinks in us so that you may illuminate our judgments of others and ourselves. Bless you for your unending pursuit of new life and light in our dead, dark places. Amen.

PRAYER OF CONFESSION [unison]

Blame is a silent and spoken ax we grind. Forgive us, Holy God. We chop people into pieces by small, blind judgments. Sometimes, we fault others to make ourselves feel better. Sometimes, we are simply mean or petty. In every case, when we strike out the possibility of new life for someone else, we cut off the chance of new life for ourselves. Stop us from doing this. May our question be not *who* is to blame, but how *we*, illumined by your presence, can help.

CHILDREN'S SERMON: Blaming Victims

Ask: Have you ever gotten in trouble and tried to make excuses for what you did — or blamed someone else for doing it or making you do it? Say you're fighting with a friend or a brother or sister and something ends up broken. When your parent steps in to find out what happened, what do you say to try to get out of trouble? [Let the kids answer . . . suggest some responses if they are reluctant to reply.] Do you ever say, "It wasn't my fault!" or "She started it!" or "He pushed me and I couldn't help it!"

Adults play the "blaming game," too. We try to make excuses to explain why things go wrong. Sometimes we do it to get out of trouble. Sometimes we do it because we don't understand how something happened, and we try to explain it by blaming something or someone else. When someone gets sick, we might say, "Oh, he shouldn't have eaten that or smoked this or worked so hard." Or, if someone is hurt in an accident, we might say, "She was driving too fast or too slow or she wasn't paying enough attention to where she was going." Other times, we blame God when bad things happen because there isn't anyone else to blame.

Sometimes, those explanations might be true. Sometimes a person *does* do something that causes sickness or injury. But when Jesus' disciples ask him who is to blame for a man being born blind, Jesus tells them that assigning blame is a silly thing to do. It is more important, Jesus says, to discover how God is at work within our limitations, changing our lives for the better, even in the middle of things that seem bad and unfair.

SERMON NOTES

Main Point: "Though I was blind, now I see." Lent is not about personal growth or self-help psychology; it is about what God does to remove our limitations and to give us new sight.

The limitations we're talking about here are not self-imposed; they are handicaps we endure because of what have been called "accidents of birth." Sometimes the limitations are physical; at other times they are the frames we put around our experiences of God and life. Like the man who was born limited by blindness, we have no control over these shortcomings.

We are all born with some such limitation, some more severe than others. Sometimes, God chooses to banish the limitation — to heal as Jesus did the blind man or to intervene in some powerful way that remedies the handicap miraculously. Because God *does* choose to act miraculously *sometimes*, we are faced with an important question. Why sometimes but not all of the time? Why did this blind man receive his sight when others did not? Why was Jesus' ministry not entirely one of healing and miracles? Why is God's miraculous intervention still apparently sporadic and selective today?

In John's Gospel, Jesus' signs and wonders are the prelude of far more important ministry. The once-blind man perceives this. In his arguments with the religious leaders, the man born blind shows profound insight, not only into what has happened to him. He perceives both the poverty of those who argue with him and the riches of who Jesus is. His theological growth and newly minted objection to the religious establishment prepare him for his final encounter with Jesus. In that encounter, after a question-and-answer session, he worships the truly Human One. Jesus leaves the Pharisees clinging to their blindness, which is their separation from God.

You might emphasize the piercing insight that accompanies any transformation God brings about in our lives. God is not content to heal, only to have us remain bound by our former limitations. Instead, God heals and then goads us along, maturing our faith to a greater wholeness than our body has experienced. The most significant healing the blind man received was when God became altogether new and personal for him. And again, God brings about this change, not we.

OFFERTORY PRAYER

Here we are — sightless, senseless, unseemly vehicles — unfit to carry your light and life into the world, dear God. Send us anyway. Send us in spite of our disabled imaginations and doubt-blinded faith. Make us life-bearers, healed and made whole by worship of you and committed to service to others.

PRAYER OF THANKSGIVING, INTERCESSION, & PETITION

Changeless Center of our lives, we thank you. Thank you for changes unexpected and undeserved, which you bring about nonetheless. Thank you for growth, written-off and long forgotten, which you sprout surprisingly in the middle of our hearts and minds. Thank you for seizing us with new purpose, radical vision, and adoring joy.

We pray for people who feel stifled or stuck — people perpetually struggling with mental illness; people constantly compromised by anxiety and fear; and people whose limitations so pain and cripple them that they have decided to write you off. Be new life to these people's atrophied places. Spring upon them with hope, joy, and delight. Inspire in them renewed faith in you, in themselves, and in others.

We ask your help for ourselves, too. Spirit of the Creator, unwind us from our tangled webs of blame. Release us from the voices that tell us we are no good. Instead, let us hear your voice speaking our infinite worth. Heal us precisely where we can not imagine health. Reawaken our sense of how precious you are in our lives. Then fill our sight with visions of you and your immediate Realm. Amen.

Fifth Sunday in Lent

Gospel Reading: John 11:1–45

CALL TO WORSHIP

[based on Psalm 130, Jerusalem Bible]

From our depths we call to you, Yahweh. Hear our voices.

Our depths differ from one person to the next. Someone may cry out for new life; another for comfort; still another for direction. Nonetheless, we all need you and your help.

If you never overlooked our sins, Yahweh, could anyone survive? But you do forgive us and for that we revere you.

In our depths we sense how separated we are from your life. We worship you because we need you to bridge the gap between who we too often are and who you want us to be. We worship you because you join us to our better selves by forgiving and giving us hope.

PRAYER OF PRAISE [unison]

Holy God, you make tombs into birth places. You raise us to faith, weep by our sides, and share our troubles. You command life to appear where none exists. You shower us with signs and shudder us with your hopes. For all you do and are, we love you. Amen.

PRAYER OF CONFESSION [unison]

One rooted in mercy and fast to forgive, we want to understand you but don't. We want to believe you but can't. We want to trust you but won't. Forgive how we falter in our understanding, faith, and trust of you. Most of all, pardon how we lock ourselves out of the countless ways you seek to bring us life.

CHILDREN'S SERMON: Resurrecting the Dead

Ask: Do you know someone who has died? [Get names from the children and remember them for a closing prayer.]

Today's story is an amazing story with a happy ending about Jesus and a friend of his named Lazarus. Lazarus has died, but Jesus brings him back to life. The fancy word Christians use for this is "resurrection." Jesus resurrects Lazarus.

Have you ever wondered what happens to people when they die? Even Christians have a lot of different ideas about what happens to us after we die.

One thing we can agree on is that, whatever happens, God makes the decisions. Whether we believe that people go right to heaven or whether they wait until God resurrects everyone, we can agree that the power to bring people from death back to life belongs to God. People don't have that ability.

Today we are going to remember people who have died. We are going to pray that they rest in Christ Jesus and will be given the life only God can give. We will also pray for those of us who are still living, but who miss those people very much. Even Jesus cried when his friend died — even when he knew he was going to resurrect Lazarus. God understands that it hurts us when we lose someone we love.

[Lead a prayer using names the children have provided.]

Dear God who has powers we don't understand, we remember _____(names)_____. We pray that you give them comfort and rest with you forever. We pray that you bring them into the new life Jesus says can be ours because you love us. We pray that you will be with us who are still alive, too, because it makes us sad when we miss our family and friends who have died. Thank you for understanding our sadness, and for being with us when we cry. Amen.

SERMON NOTES

Main Point: We like tidy pictures and answers to untidy and unanswerable questions, but the conversation between Martha and Jesus in verse 24 and following suggests that human opinions — even the truths we cull from Bible stories — fall short of God's truth. God's truth about the afterlife is not about dogmas we shape but about a Presence that shapes our futures, including our eternal futures.

Just about everyone has an opinion about what happens when folks die. We are all over the place on this. Even Christians have a wide variety of views on the subject. Some consider death a small passage to an automatically larger life. Others dabble with reincarnation. Others continue in Martha's tradition, believing in a general resurrection first, then a judgment, and then eternity.

What can we tell our congregations about life after death? We can proclaim our own opinion, what we think is the "right" answer. Or, we can try a different approach. Let me suggest an alternative.

Martha offers Jesus orthodoxy. Jesus gives Martha mystery. Jesus' statement "I am the resurrection and the life. Those who believe in me, even though they die, will live" is not a street map showing the way to heaven. On the contrary — it explodes Martha's (and our own) dogma. Jesus says to Martha, "I am the resurrection right in front of you. Not a resurrection plotted and schemed in theological treatises and arguments, but an explosion that shatters death so that life wins. I am that explosion of life. Behold everyone's resurrection."

What Christ means in practical terms is entirely unclear. What about souls, judgment, and eternal life? Isn't there a process to, through, and beyond resurrection that God monitors at least? There may be answers to these questions, but Jesus does not provide them. What he offers is better.

With the same immediacy as he declared, "The realm of God has drawn near,"

Jesus says to Martha, "The resurrection has drawn near and it is I." What Jesus proclaims is the overwhelming assurance that God's resurrection is God's immediate presence.

We may not like this lack of specificity, this mystery, but we need it. The good news is that Lent is a time for unsettling; it is a time to hear bald, brave claims from Jesus about our lives and to upset our well-worn pictures about Jesus and resurrection. Start by letting go of your own carefully and dogmatically crafted views. If you can help your people and yourself to do this, you will hear Jesus' claim "I am the resurrection" with fresh, exciting new force. The power behind that claim is sufficient to move any stones from the tombs in which we half-live and to remove any limits we have placed on what God might do.

OFFERTORY PRAYER

Here we are. Send us into mystery, which makes mayhem of human ideas. For the journey, provision us with trust that we may go to others, bearing your mysteries and Presence. Amen.

PRAYER OF THANKSGIVING, INTERCESSION, & PETITION

We thank you for mystery, Holy Center of Life, Time, and Eternity. We thank you for your unfathomable resurrection powers and promises. We are grateful for you whom we don't understand but whom we try to comprehend anyway. We are happy for Jesus' tears. We delight in how he takes away the stones that obstruct our living.

We pray for the living dead: people labeled and pronounced dead to life as we value it. We pray especially for people with schizophrenia, manic depression, psychosis, and neurosis. We ask that your resurrection presence find and pull them back into life among us.

We pray also for ourselves. Where we stink with opinion, perfume us with mystery. Where we are too content with what we know, unravel us by faith's larger life. Where we struggle behind labels others have for us and barriers that tempt us to passivity, we pray your resurrecting presence. Come and open up places within us that we have written off as dead, even our whole selves.

Palm Sunday

Gospel Reading: Matthew 21:1–11

CALL TO WORSHIP

[based on Psalm 118]

Blessed is the one who comes in the name of the Lord.

We bless you, Jesus, from the house of the Lord.

ALL: *O give thanks to the Lord, for God is good, for God's steadfast love endures forever.*

PRAYER OF PRAISE [unison]

May our praise today be soft petals at your feet, Lord Jesus, Holy Master, for with feet you walked the earthly places of this life. With tongue, you spoke of our Creator's Realm. With hands, you touched and healed the deep wounds we bear. As you blessed us with your presence then, so you bless us with your presence now. We praise you who continues to be life for us. Holy and wonderful are you. Amen.

PRAYER OF CONFESSION [unison]

Forgive us, Holy God. Our praise dies quickly. Our good intentions are fog burning off in the morning. We want to walk with you but turn aside easily. What we fail to do slides from our minds and out of our consciences. We wish to honor you with our whole lives but run for safety. Then, we offer you excuses. Redeem us. Save us from living in mists and shadows. March us into the bright and holy Realm you embody.

CHILDREN'S SERMON: Grand Entrance

Ask: If you were going to ride an animal, what animal would you choose to ride? Now, if you were the President and you were going to enter a town, what might you choose to ride in? [Limousine, helicopter, plane would be common answers and possibilities.]

In Jesus' time, a king often used a chariot and rode into towns with a whole bunch of people behind him, some of them in chariots and others on foot. People in positions of authority often use fancy ways of getting around. Jesus was very important and powerful, but when he entered Jerusalem, he did not use a chariot. Instead, he came into the capital city on a very common animal that was not at all special. Do you know what he rode? [Let them answer.] The Bible tells us that Jesus rode a donkey. He did this for two reasons. One was to show the people he was doing things like a prophet had predicted would happen many years earlier. The second was to remind all of us that what is important in God's mind is not showing off. Jesus didn't need to make a grand entrance to show how important he was. When he rode on an ordinary donkey, people still knew he was someone special. When we don't try to act important but just do what God tells us to do without showing off, we are being humble. That's how Jesus lived. It should be the way we live, too.

SERMON NOTES

Main Point: Lent is about God repossessing anything from us that God needs. Possessions were spontaneously shared on Palm Sunday. A donkey was provided. Cloaks were thrown on the ground to be trampled and soiled. Tree branches were ripped off and spread on the road. Bad ways to treat precious things. Yet, they were necessary because the Lord had need of them. What does the Lord need from us?

Many preachers get tired of Palm Sunday sermons when they do them year after year. Topics begin to feel limited. There are good reasons for adopting a "Passion Sunday" tradition to replace Palm Sunday as the day's focus. Before abandoning Palm Sunday, however, consider the following in an effort to rediscover the tradition's vitality.

Focus on the opening part of the story. The Scriptures tell us that Jesus sent two disciples ahead to secure a donkey. There is no mention of "borrowing" the animal. There is no indication that the owner had knowledge of Jesus and agreed because he or she was one of Jesus' followers. We insert these ideas into the story to fill the holes in the narrative. Consider a different approach to this episode, however.

Imagine that no promise was made to return the donkey. Imagine that the owner did not even know Jesus, except maybe by vague reputation. Then, work the story.

Imagine God entering our lives and commandeering what the Lord needs. What would God ask of us? What could we provide that would bring Jesus humbly into the world? Money? Our lives? What about possessions that are instrumental to our livelihoods? What about a fancy computer, instead of a cast-off model, given to the church office? Perhaps, your professional services given freely and quickly when asked. What about the rarest of possessions — time — time right now to take leftover food from the fund-raising church dinner directly to a shelter or soup kitchen several towns away? How would you respond if a stranger came to you and asked you for something because "the Lord has need of it"? Would we let our donkey go freely, or would we need a signed agreement for its return and damages if it were mistreated or hurt?

OFFERTORY PRAYER

Here we are — your donkeys of whom you have need. Take and use us where you will. By our plodding steps, ride silently and surely again into your world. Amen.

PRAYER OF THANKSGIVING, INTERCESSION, & PETITION

We thank you, God, for being in Jesus bigger than life. We thank you for his model, but mostly we thank you for his presence: for the many dimensions in which his words and ways speak to our weariness; for his face shining serious, sad, and exuberant; for his tender acceptance of our deepest pains; and for his pleasure in our highest joys. Thank you for parading into our lives through his flesh and bones. Thank you for nursing out of our lives his soaring Spirit.

We pray for people: for people who cheer you now but who fall away when trouble comes; for people who sneer and snipe at you; and for people who are heads-down indifferent to you. Walk surely and slowly into these lives. Help them discover discipleship, applaud you, and pop-up embrace you.

We may pray for folks who turn away from you because we include ourselves among them. Where we hide behind stout walls, ride holy and humbly through our gates. When we are quick to join a good show but quicker to run from a showdown, infuse us with your courage and determination. In your magisterial silence, ride into our lives again and again. Amen.

Maundy Thursday

Gospel Reading: John 13:1–17; 31b–35

Introduction

Various Maundy Thursday traditions flourish in our churches. For many, this evening means a potluck supper and a communion service around dinner tables. Other congregations weave a Tenebrae service onto a communion service. Some churches hold a Christian Seder, duplicating Passover and overlaying this Jewish house ritual with communion. A few groups practice foot washing. Many alternate their services from year to year.

In addition to the established worship elements, we also present a new Ritual of Washing specifically for Maundy Thursday — a variation on the ancient rite of foot washing. Its purpose is to replace the traditional offering and Offertory Prayer with an opportunity for people to present themselves for God's cleansing. Small congregations and persons who honor this day by worshiping in small groups might still consider foot washing as part of their service. The new ritual presented here is intended as an alternative that overcomes some of the obstacles foot washing presents for a large gathering of people — the practical as well as the emotional ones.

Other than the omission of the Offertory Prayer and the addition of the Ritual of Washing, the same worship elements presented for other services are included here. Although not all of the selections may be appropriate for the format your church has chosen for Maundy Thursday, it is hoped that some part of what we present can be utilized.

CALL TO WORSHIP
[based on Psalm 116:15]

The psalm says: "Precious in the sight of the Lord is the death of his faithful ones." What does this mean?

It means martyrdom is rare, and should be rare, but holy and wonderful to God, nonetheless.

Tonight we remember God's greatest martyr: God's own flesh judged and condemned, torn and trashed, abandoned and abused, even Jesus of Nazareth.

We remember him not only for what he said but also for what he did this night and in the days ahead.

ALL: *What he did was to praise God with every fiber of his being. What he did was to honor God in every breath, in spite of evil's guile. What he did, we do in our tiny way now: praise the God whom we love, too.*

PRAYER OF PRAISE [unison]

With the hands through which we put nails, you wash us, Holy One. In bathing us with wholeness, you remove partiality from human living. In you, none should be impoverished. No one should feel marred by stain or stress. Nobody should feel impure or puny. All should feel powerful, satisfied, and complete. For bathing us with salvation, we praise you. We adore your great example. Bless you who gives us to one another in love. May this be so.

PRAYER OF CONFESSION [unison]

You say we are clean; we feel unclean. We feel the soaking, sinking presence of stress and strain. We feel it in our lower backs, our headaches, and in our hurting feet. We feel more bunioned than blessed, harried than happy, and more alone than adequate. So tonight we pray that, in these feelings which mark our humanity, we will find your divinity. Fill every word and silence in our worship. Round off every thought and action tonight, that we may sense you wiping away all that makes us less than whole.

CHILDREN'S SERMON

[Do a foot washing with one or two members of the congregation. Recruit people to participate in advance, and prepare how you will actually perform the ritual in front of the children.]

Most of the time we celebrate Maundy Thursday by recalling that Jesus ate a special meal called Passover with his disciples. Then, we have Communion, remembering how Jesus shared bread and wine with his followers at that meal. This story is described several times in the Bible.

One of the stories in the Bible is different, however. It describes Jesus sharing a meal with his followers, but then it says that, instead of breaking bread and sharing wine, Jesus did something else. He washed his disciples' feet.

We are going to do that tonight. [Bring your volunteers forward and seat them in chairs facing the children.] Jesus washed his peoples' feet as an example for us to follow. We are too proud and independent to care for one another sometimes. Jesus wants us to be willing to love each other despite barriers that come between us. Sometimes, that means loving someone who is unlovable, and sometimes that means letting someone else love us when we don't feel very lovable. When we wash one another's feet, we let go of our pride and let someone else help us — even if we are embarrassed by the situation. We let go of our fears, and let someone touch us in a loving and unthreatening way.

[Perform the foot washing; you may wish to have your volunteers wash your feet as well. This will take more time than is customarily given to the children's sermon, so choose carefully how to make the most impact upon the children by not letting the demonstration go too long. You might also have the congregation sing a hymn or two during the foot washing. Many songs would be appropriate choices, but the Negro spiritual "Wash Me in the Water" is an excellent option.]

SERMON NOTES

Main Point: Briefly prepare people for the new cleansing ritual that is described below. Emphasize surprises — and how uncomfortable they can make us.

Jesus liked surprises. Washing his disciples' feet was a surprise meant to imprint an example into their minds. It did. The lectionary honors that example by suggesting this reading during Lent in each of its three years. Yet, this ritual is only sparingly practiced in modern Christian congregations. Your sermon might address why and then propose a remedy.

In a large congregation, foot washing feels impractical. We know the familiar objections.... "So many people; too much time. It makes people feel uncomfortable. Besides, Maundy Thursday is really about Passover and Communion — not this idiosyncratic story in John's gospel. Give us what we know. Protect us from surprises."

Surprises, good and bad ones, pounce upon us every day. The exciting news of pregnancy. The terrible terror of a cancerous lump. The unexpected pleasure of a birthday party. The unforeseen dread of a late-night telephone call. Surprises are as much a part of life as is our desire to minimize, control, and convert them into palatable change.

Expand upon how we try to tame surprises and why. Observe that, if done in love and as Jesus suggests both by example and words in the passage, surprises bring a creative vitality necessary in our worship. Introduce the following modern-flavored ritual as a surprise in this service.

A RITUAL OF WASHING

[This ritual, a variation on Christ's example of foot washing, can replace a traditional offering in which money is collected. It intends to give people a chance to offer themselves up to God in a wholly different way. For this ritual, you will need as many deacons or lay leaders present as you deem expedient. Each will be stationed in the front of the sanctuary with a bowl of water. Communion could follow this ritual.]

Introduction

"During the supper Jesus, knowing that the Father [Abba] had given all things into his hands, and that he had come from God and was going to God, got up from the table, took off his outer robe, and tied a towel around himself. Then he poured water into a basin and began to wash the disciples' feet and to wipe them with the towel that was tied around him" (John 13:2–5).

Ritual

Throughout his ministry, Jesus spoke and acted in ways that shocked and surprised his observers. Both in the Passover meal and with foot washing, he astonished his followers with new insights and memorable examples; in repeating his actions in the rituals of communion and of foot washing, we remember his presence — a Presence that lingers with us to this day as the Spirit who comes into our midst.

To honor that unpredictable but loving Presence, you are invited to a washing ritual. As the worship leader/choir/lay leader leads us in song, I invite each of you to come forward and be washed.

[You might make reference to their baptisms or the ritual of baptism in connection with this cleansing, especially if you involve the church's baptismal fount in the ceremony.]

This ritual should embarrass no one. It honors both our need to present ourselves to God for cleansing and our desire to be purified. As each person comes forward, a deacon or deaconess will cleanse your mind, mouth, and hands with water in unthreatening ways.

[The deacons/deaconesses will work in pairs. One will dip his/her fingers into a bowl and make the sign of the cross on three places on each person's body. The other deacon/deaconess shall recite the following words as each sign is made; speak the person's name, if known.]

[Forehead]

Holy Christ, wash and cleanse this mind. Purify her/his emotions, intentions, and interior life.

[Both cheeks, at either side of the mouth]

Holy Christ, wash and cleanse all that comes out of this mouth. May it tell truth and speak love.

[Hands, in the palms or on the backs]

Holy Christ, wash and cleanse these hands and all that he/she does in his/her life. May these hands do as you would do and his/her feet walk as you would walk. So be it.

[During the washing the congregation may remain seated and sing hymns. Depending upon the tone you want to set, the hymns could reflect a penitential mood or simply a reverential one. Some songs to consider might be: "Blessed Assurance"; "Lord Jesus, Think on Me"; "Draw Thou My Soul, O Christ"; "Just as I Am, Without One Plea"; "All My Hope on God Is Founded"; "My Faith Looks Up to Thee"; "Lord, I Want to Be a Christian"; "Rock of Ages"; "Have Faith in God"; "He Leadeth Me, O Blessed Thought"; "Be Thou My Vision"; "Lord, Speak to Me, That I May Speak"; "O Love That Wilt Not Let Me Go"; "Take My Life and Let It Be"; and "Breathe on Me Breath of God."]

Closing Prayer

Jesus says that we are clean and that we have full shares in him and his life. We pray this be so.

Our outer and inner parts are yours, Holy Christ — places for you to settle and roost, places in which your example lies quietly and from which we are moved to act boldly. We give you our inward and outward lives. Scrub them wholly and make them holy until they shine with your limitless love. Amen.

PASTORAL PRAYER

We thank you, God of comfort and surprises. By the comfort of love, you wrap us into the goodness of community. By surprise, you leap into our hearts, calling them to pump with new life and freedom. Thank you for Jesus' example. Thank you for soul scrubbing and cleansing calm. Thank you for the wholeness of fractured bread. Thank you for the fullness of the Spirit that is possible when we are poured out.

Cleanse the world from Afghanistan to Zimbabwe and America from Anaheim, California, to Zephyrhills, Florida. Purge its molding minds and stinking spirits. As you were, innocents are betrayed every day. Nameless people are dumped into mass graves. Women and children targeted for genocide. Evil tempts and confuses, and wrong abounds; righteous acts seem rare and precious. So, we pray that *you* do right by starting over again in our lives — by our choices, through our actions, and in spite of our ongoing failures of faith and spirit. May our minds, mouths, and hands flood the world with your goodness, and may your love overflow our hearts into the world. Amen.

Easter Sunday

Gospel Reading: John 20:1–18 or Matthew 28:1–10

CALL TO WORSHIP

[Note the responsive reading is divided between men and women. The men's voices are designated by regular typeface; the women's voices are in **boldface type.**]

Men: Today starts with grief, bewilderment, and surprise.

Women: **It passes through fear, incredulity, and ends in astonished recognition....**

Men: ...that something wonderful has happened...

Women: **...that something wonderful is still happening...**

ALL: *...because of the life God restored in Jesus. We come to worship a God for whom life is the Lord's last and best word.*

PRAYER OF PRAISE [unison]

God of Israel and God of us, we shout our praise to you. You bury suffering and death. You cast off the shroud of betrayal. You push aside the boulder of human injustice. You rise before us — a light in the darkness and victory in the face of death. We adore you who breaks through all that entombs us. We bless you who bursts through the gloom and gallows to grant us grace never ending. We celebrate your life which becomes the beat of our own hearts, this day and forevermore. Amen.

PRAYER OF CONFESSION [unison]

One who brings new life to dead places, we ask your forgiveness. We cause suffering for others through slicing words and slashing comments. We strip people of life because we have not been present to help them or generous enough to meet their needs. We brand and abandon people through our ignorance. We bloat ourselves with smug arrogance and chalky condescension. Bring us out of these tombs. Free us of our shrouds. Restore life to us. Then guide us along the great walk of joy you make possible today.

CHILDREN'S SERMON: Sweet Earthquake

Ask: How did Easter morning begin for you? Have you hunted for an Easter basket or dyed eggs or had a special breakfast? [Let the children relate their morning's activities.]

The Easter we celebrate today started out very differently. It began with an earthquake. Imagine the two women who were on their way to Jesus' tomb. First, they felt an earthquake. Then, when they got to the hillside where the tomb was, they discovered that the big stone, which used to block the entrance to the tomb, was rolled away. There, on top of that stone, sat an angel.

The Easter story is pretty amazing. An earthquake, an angel, and an empty tomb! The women were scared by all of this at first; they didn't realize the most amazing thing about the day. The angel told them the incredible news that Jesus was not in the tomb; he was alive! Later, the disciples found this out for themselves when they met Jesus on a mountain far from the city.

While Easter is a fun day for children because of the candy and the other special things that happen, it is even more exciting for people who believe in Jesus. Easter reminds us that Jesus is still alive and that, while his presence goes on ahead of us, his Spirit stays behind to guide us. And the world, which sometimes seems like a tough place to live, is, all of a sudden, all right.

SERMON NOTES

Main Point: Was Jesus' a bodily resurrection or not? This question continues to be a controversial issue in the church. It was on that first Easter morning, too. Consider how some of the disciples doubted. To address that issue directly, take a chance with the biblical story itself. Start Easter with your own earthquake by denying the bodily resurrection, and follow the disciples through their Easter morning to discover if their truth rings true for you as well.

The transition from Lent to Easter comes by way of an earthquake. Rolling the stone away, the angel participates in this cataclysm. God thunders us out of hunkered-down introspection. When all the shaking is done, the clarion voice of an angel slices between stone-faced soldiers and shaken disciples to launch news of God's greatest miracle into the world. Dangerous stuff. No wonder the authorities wanted it hushed up.

Preached as a matter of faith or as one article among many essential Christian beliefs, Easter tends to lose some of its power. The resurrection *is* a matter of faith, and it *is* an essential article of belief, but it is also much more. First, it is an earthquake that hurts no one but helps everybody. The Easter message can again trigger a cataclysm and then hush into the angel's message at the end. The passage, after all, is not about convincing people that the resurrection truly happened. The text reports that even some of the eleven who met Jesus on the Galilean mountain and worshiped, nonetheless doubted the man before them was truly the resurrected Christ. If those first-person experiences weren't enough to convince the disciples then, how can one sermon, eons removed from the event, be enough to persuade the skeptics among us and skeptical parts within us?

Still, we preach Easter as a challenge to the part of us that we drag reluctantly into the season and to those folks who prefer the holy day to be a symbol (like a butterfly) and not an event. So, we start with the earthquake.

Try using reverse logic. Tell people that, for the purposes of today's sermon, you will deny that God raised Jesus bodily. Tell them that the church has imprisoned a mystery in the hard articles of theology and you want the mystery back — a mystery that allows for the story to be a symbol of how life overcomes death but not proof of a bodily resurrection. You might cite some current scholarship that popularizes this viewpoint. Then, let the Easter witness itself back you out of this position.

Say to your people: If it was not true. . . . How could so many people over two thousand years be willing to die for such a belief as Jesus' bodily resurrection? How could Peter and Paul travel all over the land with such a strange and unbelievable message? How could vast human possessions and resources be invested in the construction of hundreds of thousands of churches through the ages? How can the small voice inside us still draw us to the impossible, illogical claim that God grabbed Jesus from death and breathed life into him again? The martyrs who died, the disciples who journeyed, the human riches given, and the still small voice that echoes in us — all of these exist because the resurrection is true. Jesus came back with pain in his side and love in his heart. We know this to be true not because we can capture mystery by creeds but because God works through creeds to continue the angel's voice down to this day.

In closing your sermon, recite the angel's high, holy answer to Lent and God's high, holy answer to sin and death. Use the words Matthew gives. And end with the precious claim that you will finally affirm as your claim, too: "Jesus Christ is risen; he is risen indeed."

OFFERTORY PRAYER

Here we are. Send us into a world needing reassurance and surprise. Use us as spiritual earthquakes and poignant prophets. May we tremble with a news so good that doorways spring open to your resurrection life. Through our faith and actions, may Jesus palpably permeate people's lives.

PRAYER OF THANKSGIVING, INTERCESSION, & PETITION

We thank you, Lord, for your resurrection power, bursting joyfully every day into our lives. Thank you for pulling us into new life out of places of mourning and sadness. Thank you for second chances, abrupt and happy turnarounds, and the ways you reclaim us by your life. Most of all, we thank you for the new life you tender to us today through Jesus.

We pray for people who feel life closing in upon them, especially for those who suffocate under emotional pain. We pray, too, for people trapped by useless living and careless attitudes. Redeem all your people from the pits of death into which they have fallen. Pull them from life's bottoms and let them soar into the sky.

Break in upon us, too. Send us your angels and earthquakes. Where we need to die to ourselves, resurrect us into new life in you. Then, engulf us with your wild hope and unstoppable joy. As surely as you gave Jesus life again, give us this life, too. May this be so.

Section Two

PRAYER DIALOGUES
AND ANTIPHONAL HYMNS

To Donna Schaper

— my heart is the people-voice
— her eyes are the God-voice

Introduction

This section, written by Anne McKinstry, introduces an innovative element for worship for those churches who want to add a new and creative dimension to their worship services during the Lenten season. For each of the nine services in the first section, Section Two contains both a "prayer dialogue" and a hymn. Each dialogue and hymn is designed to be read (or sung) antiphonally, with one group representing God's people (regular typeface) and the other representing God (**bold typeface**).

The prayer dialogues might also be characterized as antiphonal scripture readings. The author has artfully woven together texts from the lectionary readings in a call–response dialogue that might be used in place of a more traditional scripture reading. In general, the first two stanzas of the dialogue draw from the Old Testament readings and the last two stanzas paraphrase the New Testament texts.

The antiphonal hymns are based on the same scriptural texts and are crafted in a call–response format. The words are original and have been written to the tunes of familiar hymns. The meter, tune name, and well-known hymn title have been indicated for the convenience of both congregation and instrumentalists.

Again, the regular typeface signifies the voices of God's people while the **bold typeface** signifies the voice of God. A church might divide its congregation by gender, age, or pews to achieve the antiphonal effect. Or choose one individual worship leader, pastor, or lay leader to represent God — and vary that person from week to week. You might even ask the children to be the voice of God for the reading. There is no one right way to make use of these resources.

Each reading appears on its own page to facilitate photocopying. Please feel free to reproduce as many copies of the prayer dialogues or hymns as are needed for your service.

Ash Wednesday

I Desire Truth...

We know our transgressions, and our sin is ever before us.
Cleanse us from sin. Restore to us the joy of your salvation.
I will fill you with joy and gladness. I desire truth in the inward being.
I will teach wisdom in your secret heart.
Our tongues will sing aloud of your deliverance.
Create in us a clean heart, and put a new and right spirit within us.
I will not take my Holy Spirit from you.
The sacrifice acceptable to me is a broken and contrite heart.

We seek you daily and delight to know your ways.
Why have we fasted and you see it not? We delight to draw near you.
In the day of your fast you seek your own pleasure.
You fast only to quarrel. This will not make your voice heard.
We bow down our heads like a rush and spread ashes.
Why have we humbled ourselves and you take no knowledge of it?
Is this not the fast I choose: to let the oppressed go free, to share your bread?
Call; then I will answer: Here I am.

Sometimes we practice our religion in front of people in order to be seen.
We also pray in church so that we will be seen.
Go into your room and shut the door, and pray to me in secret.
And I who see in secret will reward you.
When we fast we look dismal and disfigure our faces to be seen by others.
Our reward is feeling important and looking good.
When you fast, anoint your head that you may be seen —
not by others, but by me in secret and I will reward you with joy.

We want to, on behalf of Christ, be reconciled to God.
Is this the acceptable time?
Now is the acceptable time; now is the day of salvation.
I have listened to you and helped you.
As your servants, we commend ourselves
in genuine love, truthful speech, and in your power.
Live as people who are sorrowful, yet always rejoicing,
as having nothing, yet possessing everything.

[Words by Anne McKinstry. From *Breathing New Life into Lent*, © 1999 by Robert E. Stowe, Donna E. Schaper, Anne McKinstry, Janet E. Powers. Used by permission of Judson Press.]

Ash Wednesday

We Come Again, As Always Unprepared

HYMN: "SPIRIT OF GOD, DESCEND UPON MY HEART"
    MORECAMBE   10.10.10.10

We come again, as always unprepared
For ashes placed upon our stubborn brows.
Come as you are, clothed in sincerity;
Just who you are with flaws, you're dear to me.

We come again, unsure of what to bring;
Always the urge to please by being best.
The gift I want, a heart of honesty,
Filled with desire to lift, to serve, to love.

We come again, like children showing off,
Missing the chance to pray, commune with you.
Go to the private altar of your soul;
There is your treasure, for you're truly home.

We come again with hopes that we will be
Warmed by your spirit, moved by wind and fire.
My gift is yours to count on and receive,
Sharing my grace, my pow'r, my love with you.

[Words by Anne McKinstry. From *Breathing New Life into Lent*, © 1999 by Robert E. Stowe, Donna E. Schaper, Anne McKinstry, Janet E. Powers. Used by permission of Judson Press.]

First Sunday in Lent

Be Gone, Satan!

May we eat of the fruit of the trees in the garden?
They are beautiful and delicious.
You may eat freely of every tree;
but of the tree of knowledge of good and evil, you may not.
We desire this tree to make us wise like you.
We take of its delightful fruit and eat.
But your eyes will be opened and you will know that you are naked;
you will know of death.

When we declared not our sin, our bodies wasted away,
our strength dried up. We will acknowledge our sin.
You are blessed, whose transgressions are forgiven,
in whose spirit there is no deceit. I will counsel you.
You are a hiding place for us; you keep us from trouble.
You encompass us with deliverance.
My steadfast love surrounds you.
Be glad and rejoice; shout for joy!

We are hungry. Will you command these stones to become bread?
You shall not live by bread alone,
but by every word that comes from the mouth of God.
We see the kingdoms of the world and the glory of them.
Can all of this display be ours?
Be gone, Satan! You shall worship the Lord, your God,
and only me shall you serve.

We know that sin came into the world through one person
and this was death to many.
As Adam's trespass led to condemnation for all,
so Christ's act of righteousness leads to life.
Does the free gift in the grace of Christ abound for many?
Many died through one man's trespass,
but many more have the grace of God.

[Words by Anne McKinstry. From *Breathing New Life into Lent*, © 1999 by Robert E. Stowe, Donna E. Schaper, Anne McKinstry, Janet E. Powers. Used by permission of Judson Press.]

First Sunday in Lent

We Suffer when We Hide from You

HYMN: "DEAR LORD & FATHER OF MANKIND"
      REST   8.6.8.8.6

We suffer when we hide from you
Our heart's untruthfulness.
Come trust my understanding heart;
Confessing will restore your health.
Please heal our brokenness.

Your love surrounds, your joy returns,
As we begin to trust.
Forgiveness heals and faith rebuilds.
Your songs express a true release.
Our song is new again!

The subtle serpent shrewdly tempts
In deserts of our lives.
And I am there, my strength, my word,
Sweet angels wait to soothe your soul.
Please stay close by our side.

There is a weight that saps our strength,
And pulls us from your love.
And there's a grace embracing you;
A vict'ry has been won, my friends.
Our joyful hearts give thanks!

[Words by Anne McKinstry. From *Breathing New Life into Lent*, © 1999 by Robert E. Stowe, Donna E. Schaper, Anne McKinstry, Janet E. Powers. Used by permission of Judson Press.]

Second Sunday in Lent

I Am Your Keeper

We lift up our eyes to the hills.
They inspire us to know that our help comes from you, our Creator.
I will keep your footing secure.
I am your keeper, the shade on your right hand.
We trust that the sun shall not harm us by day,
nor the moon by night.
I will keep you from all evil;
I will keep your life, now and for evermore.

Like Abraham, we will go to the land that you will show us.
Will you make of us a great people?
I will make your name holy.
By you all the families of the earth will bless one another.
We will go to the land that you will show us.
Will we be a blessing to others?
I will bless you, so that you will be a blessing.
I will bless those who bless you.

Are we people who are born anew?
We want to experience the kingdom of heaven.
Unless you are born of water and the spirit,
you cannot enter my kingdom. Spirit is born of spirit.
We believe that you are a teacher come from God.
We want to believe heavenly things.
I am lifted up, as Moses lifted the serpent in the wilderness;
whoever believes in me has eternal life.

We know that we inherit the life in your Spirit through faith.
It is trust in you that gives grace.
Your belief in me gives life to the dead
and brings forth wonderful and miraculous happenings.
We believe you love the world and gave to us your only Son
that we may be saved through him.
Whoever believes in me shall not perish
but have eternal life.

[Words by Anne McKinstry. From *Breathing New Life into Lent,* © 1999 by Robert E. Stowe, Donna E. Schaper, Anne McKinstry, Janet E. Powers. Used by permission of Judson Press.]

We're in a Rut, Our Prayers Routine

HYMN: "SUN OF MY SOUL"
  HURSLEY L.M.

We're in a rut, our prayers routine.
We have no spirit; can we rise?
My hills are high; they point above.
Visions of heav'n can lift, revive.

How can we grow in faith, obey;
Journey to Canaans of the soul?
As your heart learns to know my voice,
You will respond with joyful trust.

We want our faith to come alive.
Be filled with spirit, fresh and pure.
New birth is yours; my gift of grace
Flows from my love like gushing streams.

We're brand new people, born of you.
Our hearts rejoice, alleluia!
Tell of my gift and share my love;
Shout your amens, alleluias!

[Words by Anne McKinstry. From *Breathing New Life into Lent*, © 1999 by Robert E. Stowe, Donna E. Schaper, Anne McKinstry, Janet E. Powers. Used by permission of Judson Press.]

Come to the Waters

My soul thirsts for you; as in a dry land where there is no water.
You give drink from the river of your delights.
Everyone who thirsts, come to the waters.
I will pour water on the thirsty land and streams on the dry ground.
You visit the earth and water it; with you is the fountain of life.
The river of God is full of water.
Water shall break forth in the wilderness.
The burning sand shall become a pool. Come to the waters!

Why did you bring us up out of Egypt to kill us with thirst?
There is no water to drink and we thirst here for water.
Streams come out of the rock; drink abundantly as from the deep.
The river of God is full of water!
You give drink from the river of your delights,
for with you is the fountain of life.
There is a river whose streams make glad the city of God.
Strike the rock and water shall come.

Give me water that I may not thirst.
Where do we get living water?
If you know the gift of God, you will ask and receive living water.
If you thirst, come to me and drink.
Guide us to springs of living water.
Give us this living water that we may not thirst.
You shall thirst no more.
Whoever drinks of the water that I shall give will never thirst.

Lord, when did we not minister to you?
When did we see you thirsty?
I thirst. I was thirsty and you gave me no drink.
The poor and needy seek water; their tongue is parched with thirst.
When did we see you thirsty and not minister to you?
Give to the thirsty a cup of cold water.
As you did it not to one of these thirsting, you did it not to me.

[Words by Anne McKinstry. From *Breathing New Life into Lent,* © 1999 by Robert E. Stowe, Donna E. Schaper, Anne McKinstry, Janet E. Powers. Used by permission of Judson Press.]

Our Spirits Thirst for You

HYMN: "NEARER, MY GOD, TO THEE"
    BETHANY   4.6.4.6.6.6.4

Our spirits thirst for you, needy and parched;
As in a dried-up land, Where no water is.
Come to the waters all who need a cup of life;
I am a living spring watering the earth.

Are we to die of thirst in this dry land?
Can rock and sand revive, give to us new life?
Water shall flow from rock, pools rise in burning sand.
I am a river full, flowing from the deep.

Lead us, O Christ, who once taught by a well,
To living waters that quench our deepest thirst.
All those who come to me shall fill life's deepest thirst.
I am a living well, never to run dry.

Filled with your Spirit, Christ, our cups o'er flow!
How can we serve you best in our thirsting world?
When you reach out to give drink to these thirsting ones;
I am the least of these; It is giv'n to me.

[Words by Anne McKinstry. From *Breathing New Life into Lent*, © 1999 by Robert E. Stowe, Donna E. Schaper, Anne McKinstry, Janet E. Powers. Used by permission of Judson Press.]

But God Looks on the Heart

Jesse made seven of his sons to pass before Samuel.
Surely the strong son Eliab is your anointed one.
Do not look on his appearance, height or stature.
I see not as you see; I look on the heart.
Samuel took the horn of oil
and anointed David in the midst of his brothers.
Anoint David, for this is he!
My spirit comes mightily upon David from this day forward.

You are our shepherd, leading us beside still waters,
restoring our souls, even through the shadow of death.
And I lead you in paths of righteousness,
comforting you with my rod and staff.
You anoint our heads with oil;
goodness and mercy follow us all our days. You are the good shepherd.
Dwell in my house forever. Fear no evil,
even when you walk in the midst of your enemies.

How are our eyes opened? How do we now see?
Though we were blind, now we see. What did you do?
I made clay with spittle and anointed your eyes.
Do you believe in me? It is I who speak to you.
Lord, we believe. Your works are made manifest in us.
If you were not from God, you could do nothing.
I work the works of God while it is day.
As long as I am in the world, I am the light of the world.

We want to learn what is pleasing to you.
We want to take no part in unfruitful works of darkness.
The fruit of light is found in all that is good and right and true;
expose the sin of darkness.
Once we were darkness, but now we are light in you.
We want to walk as children of light.
Awake, O sleeper, and arise from the dead,
and Christ shall give you light.

[Words by Anne McKinstry. From *Breathing New Life into Lent*, © 1999 by Robert E. Stowe, Donna E. Schaper, Anne McKinstry, Janet E. Powers. Used by permission of Judson Press.]

Fourth Sunday in Lent

We Need Another Look

HYMN: "MORE LOVE TO THEE, O CHRIST"
  MORE LOVE TO THEE   6.4.6.4.6.6.4.4.

We need another look, a fresh approach;
Yes, we've lost sight of you, doing your work.
Come in from tending flocks;
Relearn your heritage.
Feel my sweet oil poured on your heads.

Soft, dripping, fragrant oil, refreshes soul,
Gives weary faith new eyes, fills us with peace.
Welcome to pastures green;
Lie down in safety here.
Dwell in my house, forever more!

Anoint with earth and heav'n, our sightless souls;
Place on our eyelids, Christ, cool moistened clay.
My love, its healing touch,
Frees you from blinding fear.
Once shadows hid; now light reveals.

Our deepest pray'r, to be children of light,
Holding your gospel lamp, lighting your way.
Beams of my goodness, truth
Shine through the fog of sin.
The lost, the blind follow your rays.

[Words by Anne McKinstry. From *Breathing New Life into Lent,* © 1999 by Robert E. Stowe, Donna E. Schaper, Anne McKinstry, Janet E. Powers. Used by permission of Judson Press.]

O Dry Bones, Hear My Word

Our bones are dried up, and our hope is lost.
Can these bones live? O God, you know.
O dry bones, hear my word.
I will cause breath to enter you, and you shall live.
Will you open our graves and raise us up?
We are totally lost and dead.
I will put my Spirit within you and you shall live.
I will bring you home into your own land.

We wait for you, and in your word we hope,
more than those waiting for morning to come.
I hear your voice; the cries of your supplications.
There is forgiveness with me.
If you should mark iniquities, who could stand?
With you there is steadfast love.
With me is plenteous redemption,
and I will redeem you from all your sins.

If you had been here, our beloved one would not have died.
But whatever you, Christ, ask of God, it will be given.
Your beloved one will rise again.
All who believe in me, though they die, yet shall they live.
We believe this. How much you love those whom we love!
When we believe in you, we shall never die.
I am the resurrection and the life.
Beloved, come out from the tomb and death. Live!

We want to set our mind on Spirit, which is life and peace.
To set our mind on sin is death.
When my Spirit dwells in you, you are spirit.
Although sin brings death, your spirit lives.
Christ's righteousness is in us; we belong to Christ.
The spirit of Christ is what gives us peace.
I, who raised Christ, will give life to your mortal bodies
through the Spirit, which dwells in you.

[Words by Anne McKinstry. From *Breathing New Life into Lent*, © 1999 by Robert E. Stowe, Donna E. Schaper, Anne McKinstry, Janet E. Powers. Used by permission of Judson Press.]

Can Our Old Bones, So Dry, So Dead

HYMN: "O MASTER, LET ME WALK WITH THEE"
    MARYTON   L.M.

Can our old bones, so dry, so dead,
Rise up, connect, and live again?
Into your lifeless form I come,
And blow a resurrecting breath.

Sin drags us down; it's like a death.
Our pray'r, our hope, your saving grace.
My heart's desire is to forgive;
The morning breaks with gifts of life.

We need you near our silent graves,
You call "come out" with our own name.
Wherever death's cold grip ensnares,
My resurrecting love is there.

Life in your Spirit brings us joy;
Loving each other and your church.
Listen again; you'll hear me say:
"I've come that you might have full life."

[Words by Anne McKinstry. From *Breathing New Life into Lent*, © 1999 by Robert E. Stowe, Donna E. Schaper, Anne McKinstry, Janet E. Powers. Used by permission of Judson Press.]

My Steadfast Love Endures Forever

Hosanna, blessed be you who comes in the name of God.
Prepare the way of the Blessed One!
Behold, your King is coming to you,
humble, and mounted on an ass, on a colt, the foal of an ass.
Behold our King comes! Hosanna in the highest!
The children in your temple cry out, "Hosanna to the Son of David."
Plaiting a crown of thorns, they will place it on my head.
My steadfast love endures forever!

We prepare your way; making the pathway straight.
We cut branches from the trees and spread them on the road.
Behold, I come to you, humble, on a colt;
coming to baptize you with the Holy Spirit.
Your disciples rejoice and give praise with a loud voice
for all your mighty works. "Peace in heaven, glory in the highest!"
One will deny me three times; he will weep bitterly.
My steadfast love endures forever!

The crowds are cheering, "Hosanna in the highest!"
The crowds are shouting, "He is a prophet from Nazareth!"
Prepare my way — the way of God.
I come to baptize, not with water, but with the Holy Spirit.
Hosanna, the Blessed One comes!
We spread our garments on the road, as you ride along.
They will put a purple robe on me; they will kneel before me, mocking me.
My steadfast love endures forever!

Hosanna, blessed be you who comes in the name of God!
You come to us, humble and riding on a colt.
Prepare my way, shout with joy!
Spread your garments, wave your palms! Cry: "Glory in the highest!"
We rejoice and give you praise with a loud voice.
If we were silent, the very stones would cry out!
Soon the crowds will be shouting: "Let him be crucified!"
My steadfast love endures forever!

[Words by Anne McKinstry. From *Breathing New Life into Lent*, © 1999 by Robert E. Stowe, Donna E. Schaper, Anne McKinstry, Janet E. Powers. Used by permission of Judson Press.]

Hosanna, Blessed One!

HYMN: "O DAY OF GOD, DRAW NIGH"
ST. MICHAEL   S.M.

Hosanna, Blessed One!
Your royal path's prepared.
My way leads to a crown of thorns.
My steadfast love endures.

Hosanna, Blessed One!
Your Twelve are close behind.
My friends will flee; I'll stand alone.
My steadfast love endures.

Hosanna, Blessed One!
Our garments pave the road.
A purple robe will mock my name.
My steadfast love endures.

Hosanna, Blessed One!
We wave our palms with cheers.
Your shouts will soon be, "Crucify!"
My steadfast love endures.

(Repeat first verse.)

[Words by Anne McKinstry. From *Breathing New Life into Lent*, © 1999 by Robert E. Stowe, Donna E. Schaper, Anne McKinstry, Janet E. Powers. Used by permission of Judson Press.]

Maundy Thursday

And Girded with a Towel

You pour water into a basin, wash our feet and wipe them with a towel.
It is hard for us to have you wash our feet.
If I do not wash you, you have no part in me.
Later you will understand this humble act of mine.
Wash not only our feet, but also our hands and head!
We know you love us to the end.
Do you know what I have done for you?
I have given you an example; wash one another's feet!

On the night you washed our feet you took bread and the cup,
blessed it and gave it to us.
Take this in remembrance of me; for you have a part in me.
This is my broken body and the cup of the new covenant.
Will all people know that we are your disciples?
Shall we wash one another's feet?
A new commandment I give you: Love one another as I have loved you.
All will recognize me in your love.

We eat your bread and drink your cup and remember you as we partake.
Have we a part in you?
This is my body for you; you have a part in me.
You are proclaiming my death until I come.
We argue as to who is the greatest.
We hear you say that the greatest among us is the servant.
I am among you as one who serves!
I have prayed for you that your faith will not fail.

We watch you kneel down and pray in the garden.
We hear you say, "If you are willing, remove this cup from me."
Listen again as I say, "Not my will, but yours be done."
Why do you sleep? Rise and pray.
We watch your agony as sweat becomes drops of blood.
There appears to be an angel from heaven strengthening you.
Pray, that you may not enter temptation.
It is the hour; the power of darkness comes.

[Words by Anne McKinstry. From *Breathing New Life into Lent*, © 1999 by Robert E. Stowe, Donna E. Schaper, Anne McKinstry, Janet E. Powers. Used by permission of Judson Press.]

Maundy Thursday

We're Ready to Receive

HYMN: "BREATHE ON ME, BREATH OF GOD"
      TRENTHAM   S.M.

We're ready to receive
Your humble servant-towel.
You truly have a part in me;
I'll bathe your tired feet.

We're ready to receive
Your gracious bread and cup.
You truly have a part in me;
I'll feed your hungry souls.

We're ready to receive
Your emptied cup for us.
You truly have a part in me;
Come taste my sacrifice.

We're ready to receive
Your midnight garden-prayer.
You truly have a part in me;
Come die, then live and serve.

[Words by Anne McKinstry. From *Breathing New Life into Lent*, © 1999 by Robert E. Stowe, Donna E. Schaper, Anne McKinstry, Janet E. Powers. Used by permission of Judson Press.]

Easter Sunday

Go Quickly and Tell

We come at dawn to see the sepulcher.
A radiance greets us, like an angel. We are afraid.
Do not be afraid. I am not here, for I have risen.
Go quickly and tell my disciples!
We run to your friends, and we find you already with them.
We touch your feet; we are afraid.
Do not be afraid.
Tell all my friends to go to Galilee; there, they will see me.

At dawn we run towards the tomb; we go into the tomb.
We see now and believe — you must rise from the dead.
Do not be afraid,
for I know that you seek Jesus who was crucified.
Like Mary we weep and look into the tomb, seeing two angels in white.
They say, "Why are you weeping?"
"My friend!" Go to my disciples and tell them,
I am ascending to my God and your God.

We depart quickly from the tomb with fear and great joy
and run to tell your disciples.
I meet you on the road to Galilee
where you touch my feet and worship me. Go and tell!
We go and tell everyone that you have risen from the dead!
We have seen where you lay in the tomb.
Go with the disciples to the mountain to which I have directed you.

We go to the mountain as you have commanded.
We worship you, but our faith is not perfect.
All authority on earth and in heaven has been given to me.
Go and tell; make disciples of all peoples.
We will teach them all you have commanded us,
preaching good news of peace, doing good, and healing.
Everyone who believes in me receives forgiveness of sins.
I am with you always!

[Words by Anne McKinstry. From *Breathing New Life into Lent,* © 1999 by Robert E. Stowe, Donna E. Schaper, Anne McKinstry, Janet E. Powers. Used by permission of Judson Press.]

Easter Sunday

At Dawn the Stone Rolls Back

HYMN: "REJOICE, YE PURE IN HEART!"
   MARION   S.M. WITH REFRAIN

At dawn the stone rolls back; Your empty tomb revealed.
Go tell my friends I live again! We'll meet in Galilee.
ALL: *We'll meet, we'll meet, We'll meet in Galilee.*

At dawn bright angels sing "Hosanna!" once again.
Go tell the poor I live again! We'll meet by teeming nets.
ALL: *We'll meet, we'll meet, We'll meet by teeming nets.*

At dawn our faith's renewed, Our name so sweetly called.
Go tell the sick I live again! We'll meet in Jordan's stream.
ALL: *We'll meet, we'll meet, We'll meet in Jordan's stream.*

At dawn your truth is clear. Our eyes, our ears are pure.
Go tell outcasts I live again! We'll meet by Jacob's well.
ALL: *We'll meet, we'll meet, We'll meet by Jacob's well.*

At dawn the stone rolls back; Your empty tomb revealed.
Go tell the world I live again! We'll meet in the upper room.
ALL: *We'll meet, we'll meet, We'll meet in the upper room.*

[Words by Anne McKinstry. From *Breathing New Life into Lent*, © 1999 by Robert E. Stowe, Donna E. Schaper, Anne McKinstry, Janet E. Powers. Used by permission of Judson Press.]

Section Three

LENTEN REFLECTIONS

To Roger Barnet,

friend and mentor

Introduction

The Lenten reflections in this section are provided by the Reverend Donna E. Schaper. Some of the thoughts will challenge and convict; others will encourage and comfort. All may be used in several ways through the Lenten season. You may choose to read through this section as part of a daily devotional time. Pastors may find illustrations and anecdotes for sermons. Many of the entries are ideal for inclusion in church bulletins or newsletters. Feel free to reproduce whole entries or excerpts in your congregational publications.

These reflections are sifted into two parts for your convenience. The first are more general Lenten reflections, while the second are loosely organized in association with themes and scriptures identified by Rev. Stowe in Section One.

General Lenten Reflections

During Lent, we try to reframe our lives, to position them inside a new picture frame, one that includes rather than excludes God. Lent is a good time to eat the bread and drink the wine of God's presence, whether in solitude on a late-winter evening or in the communal Eucharist with God's people.

Communion is a device that helps us remember that God is with us. Just a little bread, a little wine — but they are a powerful reminder to those of us who still confuse bread with stones, who think that even free gifts involve some kind of price tag. These symbols remind us that God is present with us, even after we sin and even (especially) *as* we sin.

We use symbols to draw God near, to shelter us. Shelter for the spiritually homeless is as needed as shelter for the physically homeless. We need soup kitchens for the spiritually starving. There we can serve the bread and wine.

————

"For where your treasure is, there will your heart be also."
— Matthew 6:21

Denise Levertov has observed that those of us who have just enough faith to know it exists manage to be amazed at how much life that little faith can support. Imagine if that faith were to grow! A little treasure can go a long way.

————

The spiritual goal of Lent is to admit our need for Lent. Just to admit our need. For Lent, for desert time, and for the promise contained in desert time.

————

Grant us the privilege of your companionship in any desert, and let us not be afraid to open the doors to difficulty. Be with us, O God, and grant us the courage to face what we must. Bring us out on the other side of this season as a matured and chastened people. And let our blessing be a blessing to your church. Amen.

————

Artists and photographers insist that the empty space around an object defines it as much as the colored part. The writer Tillie Olson spoke of her life as needing margin; she was crowded by the walls of her life's frame. Lent is the rearrangement of the space in which we live. It is a look at context, at the air, at how God is active in our lives.

————

A girl refused to be confirmed after fulfilling all the requirements. When asked why, she said, "If I join the church and confess my faith in God, that would change the whole picture of my life. God would be at the center, not just a corner. That would rearrange my whole way of living.... I'm not quite ready for that yet."

She understood the message of her Christian education: trusting God does change the whole picture. She wasn't willing to take that step. How often do we, like that girl, fail to trust God with our own reframing?

———

John Wesley, the founder of Methodism, observed that the Catholic spirit involves asking the right questions. "Let all these things stand by; we will talk of them, if need be, at a more convenient season; my only question at present is this: 'Is thine heart right, as my heart is with thy heart?'"

Repentance is getting our heart back right. When we sin, our hearts get out of whack. Repentance restores our hearts to a good position. We no longer feel forsaken when we repent.

———

Many Christians have developed arteriosclerosis; our spiritual heart arteries are constricted and clogged. We are in danger of experiencing cardiac arrest — sometimes because of compassion fatigue and sometimes because we fear the cost of genuine love. The cross opens our arteries; the cross makes it safe for our blood to flow again — life-giving blood, love-giving blood.

Of course, even when our life's blood flow has been restored, there are risks, but none more dangerous than arteriosclerotic heart disease. Love can hurt, it's true, but not loving will hurt more. Open-heart surgery can save us from future heart attacks.

———

A REFRAMED PRAYER

Let us laugh so much, O God, that we become Laughter;
Let us sing so much that we become Song;
Let us give so much that we become Gift. Amen.

Reflections for Ash Wednesday

Some of us ash our foreheads; others think we should and don't. Still others don't bother with ashes; we just color our spiritual lives gray.

We neither leave our jobs nor improve them, fix our roofs nor learn to live with the leaks, recovenant our marriages nor get into therapy. We go gray, boxed, stuck — and there we stay.

Ashes should not be a symbol of despair; Lent should be a season of renewal and hope. We humble our spirits today in preparation for the new life God offers to raise from our ashes.

———

When we are in trouble, sometimes we, like one possessed, thrash and scream. We strain against our chains. We blow the trumpet, sound the alarm. We practice our piety in whining and lamentation. We even have good reason to whine.

But Jesus asks us for another response, a quieter posture — one more content and more able to survive the troubles of our day. "Whenever you pray, go into your room and shut the door and pray to your Father who is in secret; and your Father who sees in secret will reward you" (Matthew 6:6).

Imagine. A secret closet of confidence, even when we are in fetters. The simple words of Jesus can free us.

———

E. B. White once described his aging but beloved wife, Katherine, as she knelt to plant bulbs in the October wind. "As the years went by and age overtook her, there was something comical in her bedraggled appearance: the small hunched-over figure, her studied absorption in the implausible notion that there would be yet another spring, oblivious to the ending of her own days, which she knew perfectly well was near at hand, sitting there with her detailed chart under those dark skies in the dying October, calmly plotting resurrection."

As we enter another Lenten season, as we prepare for the coming spring, may our ashen hearts share in the Easter hope and plot our own resurrection.

Reflections for the First Sunday in Lent

Think about yourself as a still life. Paint yourself in a favorite chair or window seat or grassy knoll. Paint yourself in. Use detail. What or whom did you bring with you, if anyone or anything? How do you size up? Is the current frame appropriate? In what condition is it? How about the matting? Does it fit? Or is the picture stranded in the margins, or are the margins stranded by the picture?

Jon Spayde, the writing instructor, says that a "good story lets in the little goblins." Let the devil into your picture. What does the devil want? Where is it — beside you? above you? below you? within you?

Keep the little goblins close by during Lent. Make their acquaintance. Get to know them by name.

Are there angels with you also? Give them a name also. Let them accompany you and strengthen you in the desert of temptations.

———

O God of dry, lonely times and God of powerful company, O God who knows the hard times and the soft times, the good and the bad, draw near. Stay close as we confront our own devils and our own deviltry. Do not abandon us, even as you did not abandon your own Son. Give us the courage to face what we must and to come out of Lent richer and deeper and more capable of the life you hold out to us. In the name of Jesus, the desert traveler who found his way home. Amen.

———

Lent invites us to open our eyes — and our hearts — to others. The more we shut ourselves off from the people on the side roads and the more we associate with the up-and-coming and ignore the down-and-out, the colder our hearts become and the dimmer our eyesight. We are called to do what Jesus did: to walk intentionally on the other side of the tracks from time to time, to wander in the wilderness, just to guarantee soft and open hearts . . . just to train our eyes to see again.

This Lenten season, walk a little way in the desert of others' lives; recognize how their wilderness encroaches on our world. And do not be afraid, for you are not alone. Christ is still familiar with the desert, and his Spirit is with you always.

Reflections for the Second Sunday in Lent

Romans 6:4 "...so that we too might walk in newness of life"

What if you wanted to become new and didn't know how? What if a new part of you was struggling to be born, to shed an old skin, to find a new way — but you felt wrapped tightly in shrinkwrap, like a package that stayed on the shelf too long, waiting to be chosen, waiting to be used, waiting to be discovered? Finally, all the customers go home and there you are, still on the shelf, still waiting. Shrunk. Wrapped.

If that picture describes you, then you are ready for Lent. You are ready for forty days in the wilderness. You are ready to put your life picture in a new frame. You are ready to be reborn into the life of the Spirit.

Jesus doesn't tell us to become like the Pharisees or teachers of the law; become like little children, he instructs us. He doesn't say, "Blessed are the confident and the competent and the independently wealthy." He says, "Blessed are the poor and the meek, the hungry and the weeping." When we find those needy and vulnerable parts of ourselves, we are almost ready to be saved. Indeed, Jesus tells Nicodemus, "Become utterly vulnerable and utterly new; be reborn, as an infant newly delivered of its mother."

Ready us, O God, for rebirth. Put us in touch with our need for you, and then send us to someone to who needs the you in us. Amen.

"A pile of rock ceases to be a rock pile," said the French writer and aviator Antoine de Saint-Exupéry, "when someone has a cathedral in mind." Our God has a cathedral in mind for humanity and for all of creation. When we reframe our lives, we need God's vision for us clearly in focus.

We are not just a rock pile. We are a cathedral in process. Ruins can be rebuilt; world-weary disciples can be reborn and renewed.

Reflections for the Third Sunday in Lent

My ten-year-old daughter accidentally locked herself in her room one Saturday afternoon. The doorknob simply fell off the door. She will tell you that she stayed in there reading Nancy Drew mysteries for two hours and sixteen minutes (but who was counting?), and she *did not cry*. She only worried about what might happen if she had to go to the bathroom.

Why didn't she cry? "Because I knew you would *finally* come home and let me out."

Were we a people of hope, we would sit with my daughter, patiently reading Nancy Drew mysteries, waiting for God to *finally* come and let us out. Throughout the Lenten season, we would be confident that God is on the way to set us free.

―――――

When Moses produced water from the rock, right in front of a disbelieving and fearful crowd of exiles in the wilderness, the miracle changed their whole picture. "And he called the name of the place Massah and Meribah, because of the faultfinding of the children of Israel, and because they put God to the proof by saying, 'Is God among us or not?'"

God is with us whether we know it or not. God is with us whether we believe or not. If we need some water for our spiritual thirst, we might try changing our picture. We might stop clinging to our doubt. We might ask ourselves in a quiet moment, "Is God with us or not?" We might ask then, "Do we *want* God to be with us — why or why not?"

―――――

The audacity of the woman of Samaria is impressive. She thinks she can have another chance. Wherever did she get that idea? From Jesus. Jesus asks for something from her; he asks her for a favor. She believes that this contact, this request is an opportunity, an invitation even; she can start anew. She can have another chance.

The writer Andrew Greeley assures us, "We are given second chances every day of our life. We don't always take them. But they are offered every day." Grace is a second and third chance — and more — to succeed at life. Why not? If the woman from Samaria can do it, so can we. Jesus has already made the first move; are we audacious enough to jump at his offer?

Reflections for the Fourth Sunday in Lent

A very popular poster says, "You are not responsible for everything; that is up to me. Signed, GOD."

A lot of us think that everything is up to us. We could not be more wrong. Most sin is tenaciously rooted in this mistaken judgment — that we "make" ourselves and that all of life is within our control. This is part of the lesson the author of Galatians tries to teach in asserting that Christ is necessary to our goodness. Without Christ, we are not able to *do* good or to *be* good, but with him, all things are possible.

I feel unspeakable joy at times, knowing that I don't have to make myself, that I am not alone, that I am held by God's grace. We are not alone but "made" by God for each other.

———

Once I heard a "failure analyst" talking about an air crash. "Some people are stupid enough to think that a plane falls for just one reason. Oh, *noooooo*. Failure comes from the systemic interaction of interacting complexities."

When things go wrong — whether at home, at work, at church — the problem is never so simple as what was said or done, but a combination of how and when and to whom and by whom — all in the context of what came before and what was expected from the future. And what is true in the negative, of failures, is also true in the positive, of successes.

When things work, they work because of the interaction of many factors. Credit and blame are not so easily assigned — and Christ tells us that hindsight is rarely so important as the recognition of God's presence, acting in the present moment to exercise grace in spite of it all.

For miracles to happen, we need to understand this work of grace as separate from the effects of our efforts. We need to watch for the interaction of grace and be faithful to do our part — just our part, but always to do our part.

Stop and pray: Just today, O God, let me be a part of interacting grace. Let me do something that no one expects me to do, and allow the healing waters to flow around me as well. Amen.

———

The offer of help in our addiction comes to us — but we are so addicted that we can't hear it. A way out of a psychological cul-de-sac is offered by our partner, and we attack at the implication that it's that "simple." The chance to take a better job with greater risks lands on our doorstep, and we refuse it on the grounds that we are wiser to play it safe. We act from blindness and from fear.

In the art of reframing our lives, we become people capable of accepting our salvation. We say, "Yes, help me!" when someone offers aid. We express appreciation when offered a way forward in our relationships and promise to do our best to embrace the gift of new beginnings. When the chance to take a risk comes, we hold our nose and jump into the water with the joyful confidence of a child leaping into the arms of a loved and trusted parent. We say yes to healing, to vision, to life.

Reflections for the Fifth Sunday in Lent

One day on a street in Vermont, we found rabbits under a sign that said "Freeeee bunies." My young children staged an immediate sit-down strike in front of those rabbits. My argument that the scraggly animals would never survive the winter fell on deaf ears. Reluctantly, I agreed to the adoption, bracing myself for the grief that would be as inevitable as the merciless winter cold.

The cold did come, but those rabbits survived. How? By growing fur as they needed it.

Our capacity for survival — and for resurrection — is like that of those rabbits. We grow fur as we need it, depending upon how fierce the winter is. Christ is that fur for us; there is no cold he cannot warm, no ice his love cannot melt. Nothing can separate from the love and life of God.

People wracked with cancer and twisted by disease may look and act like the living dead, but they *do* still live. They are able to move into a new frame in their lives — by embracing the Spirit that hovers in the oxygen tank, the wheelchair, the crutch, the medications, the radiation. That Spirit may or may not resurrect their bodies but *will* strengthen their souls.

We who look healthy may be living dead as well; our spirits may retreat into tombs of depression, despair, regret, denial. Yet the same Spirit is ours to embrace — the Spirit of Christ who calls to us, "Come out."

Reflections for Palm Sunday / Passion Sunday

A sign outside a long-established dry cleaners says, "Thirty-eight years on the same spot." Have you ever felt that way? Too many people are more bored than suffering. We wait restlessly, hoping God will tap our shoulder soon for an important assignment, only to live between dry cleaning pick-ups and school plays. Where is the cross for those of us who know we are a little dull, for those of us who have been on the same spot for thirty-eight years, trying to get clean or at least significantly dirty?

The cross is found in living deeply, meaningfully in the here and now; the call to bear the cross is an invitation to be available and used of the Lord. The same people who live on the corner of Main and Main, who bewail their boredom — these are the same people who have overlooked the rest of the laundry because they have seen nothing but the same stubborn spot, year after year after year.

We don't need tragedy or drama to know the cross. We can experience the cross by paying attention to the bigger picture in our own community. The corner of Main and Main is rarely as dull as it appears. Jesus walks the familiar highways and byways as well, and yours may be the donkey he requires, an ordinary beast of burden for an extraordinary mission in everyday life.

How many signals have I missed, I wonder? How many desperate people have asked me, in the name of Jesus, for a drink and I have refused? How many funding appeals have I tossed in the trash, only because I didn't realize they were the touch of Christ on my life? How many homeless people sleeping on grates have I walked past and not even noticed their presence?

No, we cannot say yes to everyone who is thirsty or homeless or desperate. But we can say yes to some. That's how Jesus saved people: one by one. And his witness caused others to pass along that salvation.

We are not asked to save everyone. We *are* asked to save someone. We are asked to be available to Christ in whatever guise he may be wearing. Be ready when the Lord has need of you.

———

Palm Sunday is the beginning of one of the longest weeks in history, a week that was the culmination of a spiritual journey from celebration to despair to victory. By Christ's willingness to undertake that journey, one step at a time, he saved humanity from itself. Let us follow where he leads.

———

Some people think it is discouraging to focus on sin and the cross during Holy Week. After all, the story had a happy ending! These people argue optimism over pessimism, positive over negative, victory over defeat. And they win half the argument; we *are* on our way to an awesome victory. But we, like Jesus, must go the way of the cross first.

Surely the crowds in Jerusalem on that first "Palm Sunday" were the consummate optimists, eager to participate in the victory parade — but they were just as quick to abandon and betray their champion at the first sign of hostility. How often do we, like that Palm Sunday mob, cling to our feverish optimism as a way of denying our vulnerability, our sin, our need for God that are symbolized in the cross? What makes us so afraid that, even surrounded by the grace and love of God, we still can't face ourselves?

If we hope to fully share in the joy and freedom of Christ's victory, we must also recognize that on the cross, Jesus shouldered *our* defeat. When we number ourselves among the throngs on Palm Sunday, do we also recognize our own voice crying "Crucify!" just a few days later? If not, then how can we accept the mercy tendered in Christ's dying words . . . "Forgive them"?

Reflections for Maundy Thursday

When we come to the cross of Jesus, we usually find that the cross demands more than we want to give. What can we do to befriend the cross? How can we lessen our fear of the consequences of loving God and loving those whom God loves — who, like we ourselves, are too often unlovable?

First, we must befriend our own vulnerability . . . our own scabs and warts, our own wounds. We are not so different from those whom we fear and despise. We are not so good as we like to believe we are. By recognizing that, we take a step forward in fellowship with the cross, that stark symbol of all we wish we weren't — but are. But if Christ could bear it, he who was a stranger to its guilt, surely we can embrace it and the redemption Jesus has brought to it and to us.

Teach us, O God, to befriend the cross. Teach us to befriend our vulnerability. Let the cross become the new frame for our lives. Amen.

————

Francis of Assisi once said, "Preach the gospel. If necessary, use words." Our Christian tradition is rich in traditions that endeavor to communicate the gospel message in symbols. Perhaps the most significant of these is the sacrament of the Eucharist.

Maundy Thursday is a day of symbol and communion, a day when memory was commanded. Today we remember Jesus through the holy meal of bread and wine. Sinful as we are, we are invited to the Lord's Table for a feast.

Our contemporary experience is *hunger*. We live in what Jerome Segal has called a "time famine" (TIKKUN, Winter, 1996). We are spiritually homeless people; we are spiritually starving — even in the richest country in the world. Why do we hunger, covet, envy? Because we imagine that we need more to be satisfied, in order for all to be well with our souls.

Eucharist implies a fullness of soul and a fullness of belonging. The eucharistic bread and wine are the best diet in the world, both feeding and slimming us — in the sense that we are "right-sized" after feeding on this spiritual food. Eucharist seats us at the table with God and with each other, and there in the thinnest wafer and smallest cup, we find abundant accompaniment. The little is plenty. We mature at the table where food is savored for its richness and not gobbled for its substance.

————

We come to the table as we are. We leave the table transformed. There we are fed and forgiven, drawn near by the Almighty God. Christ's farewell supper yields symbol, which yields feast, which yields forgiveness. Jesus departs from us now, but he does not leave us bereft. We know the comfort of the Spirit — and of one another.

Reflections for Easter Sunday

John 20:1 "Now on the first day of the week, Mary Magdalene came to the tomb early, while it was still dark, and saw that the stone had been rolled away."

We have come to the end of a spiritual journey, having been faithful to follow where Christ was faithful to lead. We have reframed the picture of our lives, establishing an awareness of God's at all times, in every way. We are no longer the center of our life's picture; God is. The stone of self has been rolled away, opening the way for life resurrected in the Spirit.

———

How can we trust the promise of the cross in a culture of suspicion? We hear so many false promises. Thin thighs in thirty days. Beautiful meals in ten minutes. Miracle cures for aging, for migraines, for ground-in stains. We have been tutored in disbelief, disillusioned by grand promises that remain unfulfilled. When a Messiah comes along and says life overcome by death can be restored to life again, most of respond as Thomas did: "I'll believe it when I see it."

But the promise stands. Jesus claims that he has the *power* — the power to do what he says he can do, the power to keep his promise, which is the promise of resurrection.

Lord, help us *see* it!

———

Too often, Easter is interpreted merely as a spiritual event. Resurrection is narrowed to a graveyard harvest of immortal souls. We neglect to celebrate the Jubilee of earth as well as heaven, even as Israel failed to do.

If Christ were to come today in resurrection power and glory, what debt of yours would be canceled — material and spiritual? What part of you would be made new? What death are you now living that might be resurrected today? How might our world look if we celebrated Easter's resurrection hope every day — not only in our spirits but in our real lives?

Resurrection is not only about canceling the spiritual debt of sin, of cashing in death's chips and salvaging life beyond the grave. Eternity begins *now*, you've heard it said. Do we live as if we believe it?

NEW SONGS FOR LENT

Introduction

This section offers original, never-before-published songs for Lenten praise and worship. They are provided especially for churches that like to include contemporary music in their worship services. The music and lyrics for these songs are the creative work of Rev. Janet E. Powers.

In general, the songs are simple and easy to learn. They can be performed by individuals or small groups as preservice music or during worship services. A church might choose one song to teach the entire congregation to sing at each service in order to provide a sense of thematic unity.

Born Anew

Janet E. Powers

Born Anew / 75

Healing Seasons

Janet E. Powers

Roll the Stone Away

Janet E. Powers

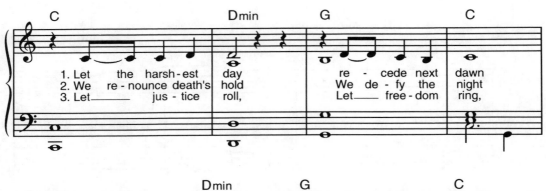

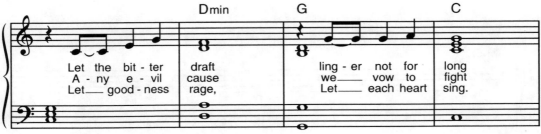

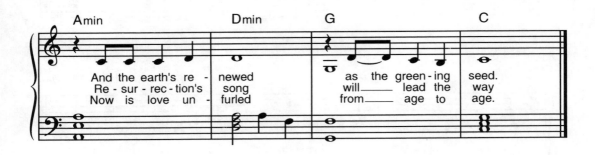

Stone and Bread

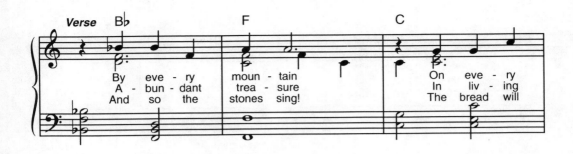

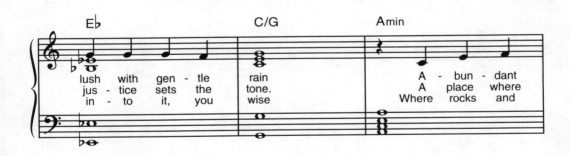

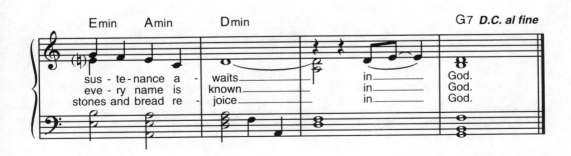

Will You Wash My Feet?

Janet E. Powers

Third Verse:
Will you sing with joy when my heart is full?
Will you dance along when I sing my song?
Will you sing with joy, and will I let you?
Will you sing with joy, in turn I'll sing yours, too.

Fourth Verse:
Will you hold my hope and passion's pride
Will you work for peace right by my side?
Will you hold my hope, and will I let you?
Will you hold my hope, in turn I'll hold yours, too.

Fifth Verse:
Will you dare to speak a justice word?
Will you set aside division's sword?
Will you dare to speak prophetic vision?
Will you dare to speak, in turn then I'll dare, too.

Your People

Janet E. Powers

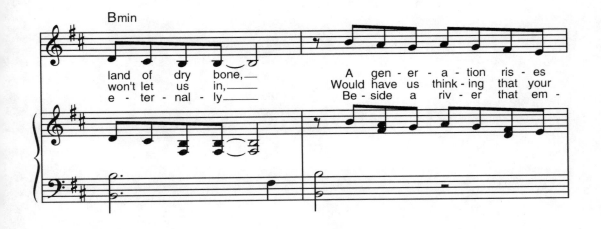

land of dry bone, — A gen - er - a - tion ris - es
won't let us in, — Would have us think - ing that your
e - ter - nal - ly — Be - side a riv - er that em -

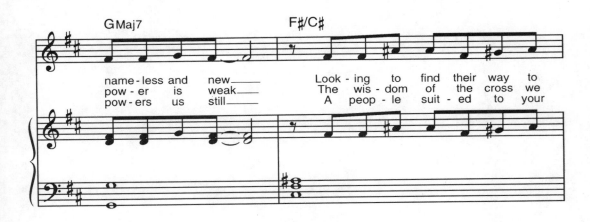

name - less and new — Look - ing to find their way to
pow - er is weak — The wis - dom of the cross we
pow - ers us still — A peop - le suit - ed to your

to Chorus

you!
seek!
will.